GOD'S GRAVITY

THE UPSIDE-DOWN LIFE OF SELFLESS FAITH

GOD'S GRAVITY

THE UPSIDE-DOWN LIFE OF SELFLESS FAITH

Craig Borlase

[RELEVANTBOOKS]

Published by RELEVANT Books
A division of RELEVANT Media Group, Inc.

www.relevantbooks.com
www.relevantmediagroup.com

Design by RELEVANT Solutions
Cover design by Ben Pieratt and Jeremy Kennedy
Interior design by Ben Pieratt and Aaron Maurer

RELEVANT Books is a registered trademark of RELEVANT Media Group, Inc., and is
registered in the U.S. Patent and Trademark Office.

For information or bulk orders:
RELEVANT MEDIA GROUP, INC.
100 SOUTH LAKE DESTINY DR., STE 200
ORLANDO, FL 32810
407-660-1411

Library of Congress Control Number: 2005911206
International Standard Book Number: 0-9768175-5-1

06 07 08 09 10 8 7 6 5 4 3 2 1

Printed in the United States of America

Dedicated to my mother, Janet Hosier. You taught me about all of this long before I realized any of the lessons were in progress. Thank you.

CONTENTS

ACKNOWLEDGMENTS

This book has been a long time coming. It started way back when I was a teenager and my mom invited homeless people to the house for summer evening barbecues. There has been too little action on my part since then, and the drive for this book comes from the inspiration of others, rather than any degree of personal achievement.

Without the people of Tearfund, none of this would be here. Over a number of years spent writing for their youth team, I have been privileged to become more educated on essential issues than I otherwise might have been. Working with Andy Baldwin, Phil Bowyer, Ben Clowney, Lorna Duddy, Suzie Gallagher, Carrie Hall, Zoe Hayes, Annie Kirke, Esther Stansfield, Anna Tattersall, Catherine Thomas, and David Westlake has been a pleasure, an inspiration, and a treat. Thank you. What's more, much of my thinking in this book was shaped by work carried out for Tearfund. Much of the second section looks at solutions and responses inspired by material I explored with Tearfund over recent years. I am grateful to the trustees for allowing me the freedom to draw on the work in this way. Above all, though, what impresses me about the Fund is the energy, passion, and commitment of the British supporters and the international partners. Seeing faith put into action in this way is truly inspiring. Take time to poke around their site at Tearfund.org and see what all the fuss is about.

There are other people who have influenced this book. Friends like John Trent, David and Minu, Mike P., Hutch, Graham Dale, and the Russells all spring to mind for a hundred different reasons. Mainly, you've been interesting people to spend time with. Thank you. Liam, Andy, and Vincent ask the questions that test my own thoughts, which is a good thing. Thanks are also due to mother-in-law Pat for introducing me to the Jonathan Sacks book, and father-in-law Hugh for letting me write about him. To Alice and Paul, I owe much gratitude for the prospect of a seemingly eternal Aussie summer that made writing through the English autumn and into the winter bearable. As ever, I owe more than I can express to my wife, Emma. You continue to push me to do better—but in the nicest ways—and continue to display an honesty that makes your encouragement so valid.

I think I will always remember the first time this book took a step toward life. It was in the office of Jeff Jackson at RELEVANT Media Group. I miss working with you, Jeff, even though our time together was short. Thanks for the sparks and the trust. Then there are the good people at Strang Communications, whose support and hard work with the William Seymour book enabled this one to find its way to the surface so easily. Of course, Mark Sweeney deserves huge thanks—for sticking with me through my confusions, for helping hone the idea, and for being far more than an agent needs to be.

Lastly, I am grateful to Cameron, Cara, and all at RELEVANT Books. Thank you for the trust and the time. Thank you for seeing this stuff as important and taking a risk to tell others.

PART 1

CHAPTER ONE

The Irresponsibility of Self

If it didn't have so many syllables, I get the feeling that some of us would consider *responsibility* a four-letter word. As a concept it is a tough one. It is associated with taking care of unruly cousins, mopping up spilled juice, or keeping tidy a room that refuses to be tamed. It makes me think of a French exchange student I once spent a month with. Her mother complained that I was irresponsible because I wanted to take a train into Paris with some other friends. I didn't like their dog, either. So being responsible in Savigny-sur-Orge seemed to me like a particularly flea-bitten, slobbery, and tedious exercise. But I had no power to resist, so I simply stayed in and felt miserable in a responsible sort of way.

The theme of our struggle with taking on responsibility stretches beyond Parisian suburbs, all the way back to the Bible. From the moment God asked the murderer Cain where his brother was, the scene was set. Of course, God knew that Abel's corpse was lying contorted in a field; He could hear the blood as it eased into the parched soil. But the question was posed nevertheless. Cain's answer, famously evasive, remains even now like some kind of eternal marker in the sand:

"'I don't know,' he replied. 'Am I my brother's keeper?'" (Gen. 4:9, TNIV)[1]

We resist the pull of responsibility. We shrug it off like so many awkward garments, twisting like preteenagers forced into formal clothes for a family wedding. Is someone else's misfortune our concern? Is it up to us to work on his behalf, regardless of whether we have been part of the initial problem?

It is tempting to write that we live in a culture that validates our rejection of responsibility. It's tempting because it is partly true. We live under the banner of freedom and independence, of being empowered to make personal choices, of taking control of our own destiny. These are good words, too, seductive words—the sort that can read like a brochure for a particularly impressive product. Of course we want to sign up for this type of life. Who wouldn't relish the opportunity to craft a decent future for himself?

The trouble is that in our hands, these concepts of empowerment and freedom and independence become stale, pale reflections of what they should really be. We make them into our own personal Christmas elves, there to serve our own needs and nobody else's. Everything becomes about us. We're supposed to be able to have the kids and keep the career, to have the career and keep the marriage, to have the marriage and keep the freedom, to have the freedom and keep the kids. It's all about us, barely ever about anyone else.

But while it's tempting to blame all this on contemporary culture, it is also wrong. Just like with Cain's bluffing, the authors of the Bible have known the eternal truths about the human condition. The pages tell a story that spans a millennium and more, with regular guest appearances by selfishness, obstinacy, and pure pigheadedness. David, Samson, Jonah, and others found themselves tripped up and spitting dirt because something inside of them placed their own desires above another's. Whether it was killing, romancing, or hiding, they had moments—some more than others—where they refused to see the link between their actions and the fate of others.

So we have an innate talent for selfishness. Big deal. I can hear my spiritually skeptical peers exhaling with gentle force once again, their eyes twitching heavenward as they prepare for another diatribe that they will put down to Religious and Middle-Class Guilt: *There goes another nice Christian getting all stressed because he thinks he needs to change the world but knows he's just as selfish as the rest of us. Why do they continue to beat themselves up about things they know they cannot change? After all, didn't Jesus Himself make some point about the poor always being with us?*

It's true. I feel responsible about this sort of thing—guilty, even. I know that guilt is not quite so hot right now, that its glory days when it was big existed way back in the Middle Ages. But waking up to the realization that we are wandering away from God's plan is no bad thing. Cain's story shows a man who is numb, or at least able to suppress his conscience, even when directly questioned by God. He resists the power of the Almighty, lies to His face, severs any guilty feelings, and wants life to carry on as usual. Even when God informs him of his punishment, Cain is still self-obsessed, claiming, "My punishment is more than I can bear" (Gen. 4:13). There is no sign of repentance, no indication that he has moved on from his earlier indifference. At least a little guilt would indicate progress. But there is none, and Cain is left to wander and struggle, his descendants only lasting until the flood wipes the board clean and the world starts all over again.

Some stories about the Church not quite getting it

I think it was early on in 1995. I can remember looking out the church window at five past six in the evening and seeing that the sky was already dark. Pressing up against the locked door, illuminated by the parking lot lights, were the people. Lots of them. They were there for a Thursday night meeting, and they were early. Things wouldn't kick off for another hour or so, but the demand for a seat had caused people to arrive earlier and earlier. So the doors were kept locked while the final preparations were made. After all, once they came in, things tended to get a little out of hand.

It had been a strange year. Twelve months before we'd heard rumors of strange things happening at a church at the end of a runway in a Canadian airport. Now we knew it was for real. The church was packed, meetings were chaotic, people were traveling from all over just to get close to the action. Best of all, as we so often said, God was showing up.

I remember the people waiting outside the church that evening. It must have had something to do with the glass and the lights and the reflections playing their tricks, but they all had a kind of morbid quality about them. It was as if they were lining up for an audition as slow-moving extras on a ghost train ride. In an hour they'd be a heaving, jumping, falling, singing, swaying, groaning mass. But as they waited, they just looked rather tepid. Maybe it felt strange having to wait outside the locked doors of a church.

WE'RE PART OF GOD'S SUPPORTING CAST, HERE TO JOIN IN AND SIGN UP TO FIGHT HIS BATTLES, RATHER THAN PICKING OUR OWN AND EXPECTING HIM TO CLEAN UP.

Ten years later, I still remember that moment before the doors were opened and the commuting congregation was allowed in. It has nestled into my memory as a defining moment, the only image needed to remind me of a simple fact: this church was on fire. This was what we had been waiting for. The buzz of expectation had become so strong that thousands of people had come through the doors during the previous months. Their own stories combined to become an overwhelming body of evidence. Lives were transformed, people rediscovered a passion for Jesus, hearts were plugged into the power—and nothing would ever be the same again.

It wasn't just us, either. There were plenty more churches around the United Kingdom doing the same thing. And beyond our borders it seemed as if every continent was in on the act. Our national press was intrigued and bewildered as we notched up the air miles to be a part of this pulsing, spreading, astounding move of God's Spirit.

Yet something wasn't quite right. There were the usual dissenters, the embittered and emotionally constipated critics pouring scorn from the side, but there were others who had questions, too. You could read the reticence between the lines of what was said by those up front. They encouraged people not to focus on whether they shook, fell, or barked during the meetings, but rather on the change that would result from their encounter with a living, powerful God.

"It's not how you go down that counts, but how you get up."

I can't even remember who said it first. But it was so true and so often repeated, it quickly became clichéd. The leaders had a point, though.

My mom had been a part of the church for years. She was, and still is, a passionately charismatic Christian. She believes in the power of the Holy Spirit and fiercely advocates the type of faith that is guided by God, subordinate to His power. It's worked for her, too; along with a growing collection of others, she has set up a local charity that has transformed hundreds, even thousands, of lives. Homeless, drug- and alcohol-dependent, lonely, forgotten people: they've all seen God's love in action through her work.

So I was surprised that she was annoyed with the church. I'd never heard her say a bad word about her fellow believers, but as I watched the line filter through the now-opened doors, I remembered the frustration she'd expressed earlier that day. The charity was going well, but the winter was proving harder than expected. The temporary night-shelter for the homeless was going to run longer than predicted, and new volunteers were urgently needed. Several local churches agreed to help out, and took on responsibility for staffing certain nights. Our church had picked Thursday, the same night as these meetings. Pretty soon the uncomfortable truth became clear: hardly anyone wanted to help out at the homeless shelter when they could be surfing on God's love and power at church instead.

> "The world is a dangerous place, not because of those who do evil, but because of those who look on and do nothing."
> —Albert Einstein

One of the few who did sign up to help was Hugh, the man who would later become my father-in-law. He's a good man with a quiet, slightly off-centered faith. He doesn't shake or sing or prophesy eloquently in multiple languages. But he's given stacks of his Thursday nights ever since to sit and talk and generally be a nice guy to an ever-revolving carousel of society's rejects. Ask him why he does it, and he's not even that sure himself. I think I asked him about it once, but I can barely remember his answer. It was something along the lines of helping because he could. Or because he should. Or because he likes them.

So, a decade on, and Hugh's still on the roster. The meetings have long since closed down, so long ago that I can't even remember when the flame was finally declared too small for us to gather around it. These days when the Toronto Blessing is mentioned, it prompts mixed reactions. Some pine for it; others snort. I heard that Jackie Pullinger brought up the subject among a number of Christians over a series of visits a few years back. She told them the story from her perspective, of how over in Hong Kong, amidst the drugs and the gangs and the death, they had all heard of the phenomenon that was taking place.

"Rich Christians were jumping on airplanes to visit the place where the laughter was," she said. "We thought to ourselves, *It will only be a matter of time before they board airplanes to visit the places where the crying is.* We waited. But you didn't come."

I didn't go, either. I just stayed home.

But something did begin to change. Slowly I began to wonder about a concept I'd previously barely heard of. Social justice sounded a little bit sketchy, especially when my ears wrapped around it at the age of twenty-one. A bright, quick-thinking fellow believer mentioned it in passing, saying something like, "Of course, without the drive toward social justice from the Church, slavery would have taken far longer to be abolished."

I looked blank. It sounded odd. I had images of people sitting around, smoking pipes and wearing home-woven blankets while sharing herbal tea with strangers. Even when the concept was eventually forced through the soggy mush of my brain, I still felt little more than vaguely intrigued. So Christians could be involved in making the world a better place by caring for the sick, the poor, and the oppressed? Sounded okay, but it never really seemed like a very impressive way to go about things. Surely, I thought, what really counted was being on fire spiritually? Surely God liked the kind of things we did in church far more than those earthy, well-meaning activities that took place away from it?

Coming around to reality was a gradual process. Many of my sacred cows had to be torn down—like believing that Christians were at their best when they were surrounded by their own, doing the things that other people thought were incomprehensibly odd. Seeing the change in temperature within the Church around 1995 was one of the final hurdles. As passionate believers allowed their faith to become ever more introverted, as leaders expressed frustration and homeless charities remained stranded through lack of support, it was clear that something wasn't right.

A few years ago, Hugh told me a story over Sunday lunch. He'd just gotten back from church, where he'd been talking to a fellow longstanding member about the actions of another local church. They were planning on setting aside a weekend where they would all descend on some local projects. They'd clean, clear, scrub, dig, play, help, lift, or do whatever was needed to improve the quality of life for the residents. Hugh reckoned it was a good idea.

"Oh," said his friend. "Well, I don't think we're quite ready for that sort of thing around here."

Over lunch we talked about the reasons why such a statement was true. We came to one conclusion: putting faith into action, seeing service as spiritual currency, simply didn't make sense to the man. He was right. He and many others in the church weren't ready for it. Why? Because the link between what they believed and what they ought to do about the surrounding chaos of poverty and oppression had not yet been formed. Put another way, they simply did not feel that offering practical help to other people was their responsibility.

Putting faith into action

So human nature struggles to wake up to a sense of responsibility. I struggle with it. My lifestyle tramples on the poor. Even now, as I sit at my desk, I consume resources without giving much thought to the impact. I can watch *Hotel Rwanda*, feel stirred to give a little money, but then forget about it the next week. I can feel the pull toward what I think is high on God's agenda, but then daydreams about cars and houses and holidays drag me back to what I fear is my default setting: thinking about me, and me alone.

But there are things going on that give me faith. There are people I meet or stories I read that tell me that things do not have to be this way. I gain faith when I see believers using their own faith as fuel for action. Some in the Church have been at it for generations. There are the Wilberforces, the Wesleys, and the Lincolns,[2] great believers and disciples of Christ who joined their faith and the injustices of the world around them. There are others too, more recent examples, like the ten thousand teens and twentysomethings who give up their summers to get on their knees and serve inner-city people and show God they're serious about the fine words they sing in church.[3]

THERE ARE A BILLION REASONS FOR GOD TO GIVE UP ON US, YET HE SIMPLY REFUSES TO DO SO.

Three months ago I was standing in a crowd at a rally. I'm not much of one for either crowds or rallies—I get kind of claustrophobic and self-conscious all at the same time—but this one was different. It was July 2, 2005, the virtual eve of the G8 summit, to which the world's most powerful leaders had traveled in order to discuss the most pressing global problems. The gathered masses were hoping to do something remarkable too. They wanted to "make poverty history." Over the previous few months I'd heard these three words variously described as insane, arrogant, miraculous, and essential. I'd forgotten how many times I'd written about the need for more aid, zero debt, and fairer trade. In truth, I'd become a little numb to it all. No big deal, you understand, but standing there in the crowd, thinking about whether there was a toilet nearby, I started to wonder why I had come—was it to join the thousands here to march or was it to observe?

It took far too long to squeeze out of the mass of people, but since I'd decided I was there to observe and not to march, it made sense to place myself on the sidelines. A couple of hours passed as I watched the people inching forward toward the march. There were a couple of others like me, sitting apart, watching—but everyone else seemed determined. Their patience put my lack of it to shame.

So I moved off to the other end of the sprawling park, where the first marchers were returning. They had that usual post-event glow about them. I continued on to a venue in the corner of the park run by some friends. More snatches of intrigue turned my head: a girl from Malawi addressing a small crowd outside Speakers' Corner, sharing her gratefulness for all the thousands who had made the effort that day; a farmer from Burkina Faso sharing through a translator that he had no education, walked nine miles each day for water, and was grateful for the help received so far; a bunch of white actors playing Africans betrayed by the West and all but destroyed by poverty.

Observing generally has a few benefits. But sometimes you have to put down the defense of the notepad and stop writing about what others are doing. For what it's worth, I went back to wait in line for the march—by then a little smaller—and took my place on the streets. It was then that I felt something strange, something only vaguely familiar: I felt proud to be there. Not because of what I'd done, but because of all the others who have defeated cynicism and suppressed the urge to be mere observers. The news came across the public address system: double the number of expected people had shown up, as many as 225,000. You know what else? I felt so proud of my fellow Christians, too. This was not exclusively a church event, by any means, but it seemed that many—perhaps even most—had shown up because of their spiritual beliefs. More banners proclaimed Christian allegiance than not, and an overwhelming number of T-shirts bore the logos of Christian charities.

There was a time when I would have felt awkward to be among such company. In fact, there was a time I *really* felt that way. It was during an event called March for Jesus, and I kept my head down the entire time, hoping no school friends would recognize me. Now, though, I was just proud. For once, the Church was making its voice heard on an issue of profound, universal importance. And the world was watching ... although not too closely. It was the day of the Live 8 gigs, a tremendous spectacle that overshadowed the march I'd attended in Edinburgh. It felt almost right that things had worked out that way, that the voice of the Church was not taking center stage. The numbers that had shown up were impressive, but Christians standing up for justice should not have been regarded as something remarkable. They were just being responsible.

The two types of responsibility

Earlier I mentioned *Hotel Rwanda*, a film about one man's fight to save the lives of innocent victims caught up in the genocide that left a million Rwandans dead over the summer of 1994. Shamefully, we in the Church largely let this horror go unchecked. We did not march or write or shout about it. Many of us were too busy getting on planes to visit the places where the laughter was.

But that's not the point I want to make about *Hotel Rwanda*. This movie will forever be paired in my mind with *The Passion of the Christ*. Both are uncomfortable films; both are essential to prick the conscience and wake us up. Both are about responsibility. Paul Rusesabagina assumes responsibility for the lives of fleeing Tutsis, offering them refuge in his hotel at great personal cost. Christ

1 MILE:
The distance the Live8 crowd stretched along Philadelphia's Benjamin Franklin Parkway

3 BILLION:
The number of people who watched the Live 8 concert

$10 BILLION:
The amount of annual debt cancellation needed to help developing countries achieve the Millennium Development Goals[4]

assumes responsibility for our sin, offering payment of His own life on the cross.

These two films have been connected for me ever since I read *To Heal a Fractured World* by Jonathan Sacks, chief rabbi of the Commonwealth and Britain. In his book he describes the presence of justice within the world, dividing it into two categories: divine and human. The divine, he says, is God's prerogative. We cannot force it, emulate it, or recreate it; it is above and beyond our comprehension and our prediction. But human justice—now that's another story altogether. Only we can create it; only our hands can make it. Schindler, Rusesabagina, Theresa—the three of them have taken our breath away with the way they have dispensed human justice, and it remains a wonderful, glorious thing whenever the least of us offers up the smallest, frailest quantity of the stuff.

But human justice is hard work. It demands that a price be paid, and it comes without that concrete, identifiable reward or receipt. That is why Hugh's friend simply wasn't ready for it. After all, why bother with human justice when you can pray and praise and sing and leave it all up to God to hand out the divine variety?

It's tempting, undoubtedly. But we ignore everything that God chose to reveal to us about Himself if we declare human justice off the menu. We need it, desperately, because creating a billion-piece set of automatons was never part of creation's agenda. We were made "in His image," destined to reflect the character of the Creator. And what can be said about that character? He is involved, intimately, and demands that we do likewise.

The narrative of the Bible screams at us from every page: We are meant to be involved. We are meant to act. We are meant to be agents of social justice on the earth. We are meant to assume responsibility for our part of the deal. Of course, the divine stuff we can leave up to God—but the human part is fully up to us.

To return to Rabbi Sacks for a bit, he makes a fine explanation of this when he looks at Genesis 18. There we read of how four thousand years ago, God sent three visitors to tell Abraham that his aging wife Sarah would conceive. With the guests about to leave, the scene shifted direction. God considered the depravity of the nearby city of Sodom and considered destroying it. Then Abraham bargained with the Almighty, seemingly bending His arm, getting God to agree that if fifty godly people could be found, the city would be spared. God agreed. Abraham said, "What about forty-five?" God agreed. Forty? Okay. Thirty? Yes. Twenty? Fine. Ten? Go on, then.

What happened next? The angels visited the city, the citizens tried to rape them, and only four decent, righteous people were found. The city got destroyed, just as God had suggested it would, even before Abraham started bargaining.

Here's the question: why did God let Abraham go through the negotiations? As the omnipresent Creator, the all-seeing, almighty One, surely God knew that Abraham's figure of ten was too high and that the city would end up trashed anyway. Why go through the motions?

Here's the answer: God wanted Abraham to ask, to get involved, to care about the state of his fellow man, because that is precisely how we've been made. We're not here to soak up the blessings and ignore the responsibilities. We're here to offer an accompaniment to God's divine justice: human justice. We're supposed to get involved; we're supposed to care, to feel, to ask questions, and to rage against the machine of a world plagued by the marks of the fall.[5]

The rest of the Bible continues the theme: God offers relationship with His created beings, and we flip-flop between responsibility and apathy, between bringing blessing and being trapped by our own selfish desires and fears.

Where do we go next?

These days I'm proud of the pockets of believers I can see solidly handing out human justice to those in need. Of course, there are those who do it without the spur of faith, a clear indication to me of just how fundamental a part of our genetic makeup such acts are. After all, when we are made in the image of God, we are clearly going to reflect His character, despite the fact that some might not be aware of where those genes originated.

But what we are doing is not enough. The world continues to be scarred by inequality; the poor continue to die simply because of their economic vulnerability; the planet revolts at the way we manage it. And who is responsible for making a difference, for opposing the

THE IRRESPONSIBILITY OF SELF

chaos? God takes care of the divine part, but what about us? Are we going to step up and be the agents of human justice? Are we going allow ourselves to become sensitized to the pull of responsibility? Or will we stay silent, leaving it to someone else, telling God that it's not up to us?

This is a book for all those who think that justice doesn't matter. It's a book for those who think it does, too. For the

Proverbs 18:5
It is not good to be partial to the wicked and so deprive the innocent of justice.

rest of you who do not yet have an opinion, read it and see what you think. Wherever we start, the journey toward responsibility has yet to be finished. Wherever we've been, past failings and successes count for little in the face of the King. Wherever we float, we can always relinquish a little more of our lives to the power of God's gravity.

THE VALUE OF GIVING

....

Ana and Ernest. Benjamin. Joyce. They are farmers, a former president, and a mother. Their stories remind me of the obvious and the not-so-obvious. Obvious that the world is small and that our actions count. Not so obvious because international aid is mostly talked about with plenty of zeros at the end of incomprehensible figures. It all seems so grand and impersonal. But at the end of the day, each of these stories would be remarkably different if not for the simple act of giving.

....

ANA AND ERNEST

Ana and Ernest, two farmers from Tanzania, know just how much help aid can bring. Living in Uhambingeto, they have experienced plenty of hardship. Droughts like the one in 2002 that left fourteen million people across southern Africa facing starvation also affected them. But along with their fellow villagers, they have benefited from money that can help finance loans and community-building projects. So far this money has produced a water tank and a medical dispensary.

According to Ana, these things have made life better:

> Before the installation of the water supply, we were spending a lot of time walking to fetch water. We had no time to do other developmental activities. The dispensary is here, but before that, many were dying. People were going back to the old ways of healing themselves by using herbs and traditional healers, so they

were in danger. But now, with this revolving loan fund and the installation of the dispensary and the water supply system, I think that we have moved a step forward. I managed to farm and get crops, then sold them and started getting money. I bought and sold piglets, as well as a bicycle and a big bag for traveling.

But Ana and Ernest's lives remain hard. By their own admission they are peasants, part of an army of the global poor whose lives can be turned upside down without warning. Droughts, floods, earthquakes, famines, preventable diseases ... the list of predators is long, frighteningly long, if you have no possibility of preparing for their arrival.

According to Ernest, while he and Ana concentrate on surviving day to day and month to month, the ability to secure a better future seems far away. Further away than Ana and Ernest would like.

"I have no idea if the government can assist us," he says. "It is very quiet. It has done nothing for us here."

But Ernest's wisdom and faith are strong.

"I am very thankful to God that I am not rich," he says. "I am poor. But I am relaxed with my poverty. I know that I would have liked to be a richer person, but I cannot be. I decided that I should keep on farming, and I have been growing maize. Even if it is not on a large scale, at least I have some food at home with my wife. Whatever I can get, I sell. If I don't get it, then I just give thanks to the Lord."

The simple truth is that aid can save lives today and build better futures for tomorrow. It can help with immediate crises as well as the essential long-haul work needed to rebuild communities. More and better aid is one of the keys to a fairer world, one in which we don't have a person dying every three seconds simply because he happens to have been born into poverty.

FORMER PRESIDENT MKAPA

According to Benjamin Mkapa, the former president of Tanzania, the way forward is clear: in order for his country to fight poverty and win, all debt must be wiped out.

Addressing the members of the Jubilee Debt Campaign in 2005, the president described the achievements Tanzania had made with the debt relief they had already received, including the construction of more than two thousand schools and an increase in primary school attendance by 50 percent between 2000 and 2004. He then outlined detailed plans for secondary education, improvements in health care, and water provision that could save thousands of lives. But there's a catch: without the cash, little progress can be made. "Give us the tools, and we will finish the job," he said.[6]

Currently Tanzania spends $120 million every year on foreign debt repayment—$120 million that could be spent saving lives and building hope for the future.

He quoted examples of things they could do if this money were released by debt cancellation. For one, they could combat malaria, the major disease threatening Tanzania. "The annual cost of treating malaria in Tanzania is $23 million, while the entire government budget for medicine is $30 million."

Not everyone is in favor of canceling debt, although unsurprisingly, the opponents all seem to come from the wealthiest countries. President Mkapa has heard their arguments but knows the true story behind the issue:

> Opponents of debt cancellation and increased overseas development assistance will tell you Africa does not have the capacity to absorb substantial new resources. They will tell you the problems of Africa are not just about money. I agree. It is

not only about money. But I am here to tell you that there are today more African governments than ever that have put in place all the other requirements for more robust growth and faster poverty reduction, such that with each new injection of financial resources, progress can be seen on the ground.

It seems that countries like Tanzania are ready to move on and deal with the cancer of poverty. The question is, will we hand over the final piece of the puzzle?

JOYCE MBWILLO

Joyce has seen firsthand the benefits of debt relief throughout Tanzania. But the story is far from over.

"It is very easy now to take my kids to primary school," she says. "They are attending primary school. It is helping them because when they come here, I know they can write. They can read. They know something about our country. But I don't think we can manage to send them to secondary school, because it is very expensive. We are not discouraged yet. We still think that the Lord will open the doors for us when the kids start attending secondary school."

Joyce understands how important it is for people like you and me to take up her cause, to decide to campaign on her behalf. She knows a Western government could help.

"We have been seeing that some of the problems are being reduced by these programs from the diocese, but we still need more systems. I would ask the government to send some assistance to Tanzania—but assistance that can reach the people at the grassroots, like here in Uhambingeto. We have maize, but we sell our produce here in the village because we can't take it into town. But the government could come here and make sure that it has given money to the Tanzanian government to improve our roads here in the villages, to enable us to have access to town, and especially to the markets."

A CHALLENGE

You may know a lot or a little about international aid. The basic story is that back in 1970, the United Nations set a target for all developed nations that would make a huge difference to the amount of aid available. They suggested governments give 0.7 percent of what they make each year. Not much, huh? Sadly, virtually all members of the United Nations are a long way from the target. Can you show them how it's done? Will you commit to giving an extra 0.7 percent of your income to directly support overseas development? Would you be prepared to give away two cents for every three dollars you receive to support long-term projects that rebuild the lives of the poorest communities?

CHAPTER TWO

The Problem
with Our Planets

I never really understood what was going on in my physics lessons.
The teachers used to attempt to stoke the interest of people like me,
standing on desks and kicking soccer balls or letting us play with
magnets, but my face and mind always remained a little on the blank
side. The one chance they had of sending a flicker of interest across
my teenage features was teaching me about space. But there just
wasn't room for all those planets and photons and quasars and quarks.
My mind, so it seemed, was too young for the feast. So it was back to
the soccer balls and magnets and daydreams about men in white lab
coats holding holograms of the solar system in the palm of their hand.

Of course, I was never going to get my head around space. Even
the great minds of our time are forced to resort to making educated
guesses when it comes to many of today's great questions. For
the ones making the news these days, it's still mainly theory and
conjecture, scribbles across a fourteen-inch screen in an attempt to
explain the boundless mysteries of the universe. But it still fascinates
me, still makes me wonder about what lies beyond our feeble
understanding.

Like gravity. The soccer ball, propelled by the faded suede boot of my
teacher, was meant to illustrate the simple fact that as a force, gravity's

pretty reliable. We can see it in action, feel it, even measure and predict it. We know that the farther away from a planet we travel, the weaker its pull will be. So if we could stand on the sun's surface—and I know that's a big "if"—the gravity there would be twenty-eight times stronger than that of the earth.

There's only one way to escape gravity: speed. To break free of the earth's invisible arms, an object needs to be punted into the air at a colossal seven miles per second. This required initial speed is called the escape velocity, and you won't get a Nobel prize for figuring out that the bigger the planet, the faster the required escape velocity. So to leave Jupiter behind, you would need to be traveling at a speed of thirty-seven miles per second. Of course, the sun's a different story altogether, requiring a sendoff velocity of more than four hundred miles per second.[1]

As the speed of light is 186,000 miles per second, it's easy to see that a black hole would need to have some hefty mass in order to have an escape velocity from which even light could not flee. In fact, a black hole would have to be a million times heavier than our sun, which would be like comparing a bowling ball to a grain of sand.[2]

Yet scientists think that black holes do exist. It's all guesswork—albeit done by ridiculously clever people with exceptionally sharp minds—but the basic assumptions about these dark anomalies are pretty much universally accepted. With all their mass and gravitational pull, they lose no light, energy, or mass. The event horizon, the boundary beyond which nothing can escape the black hole, may only be a few miles across—yet crossing it would be a deadly mistake.

It is not hard to see the work of the divine Creator at the heart of the universe. With all its mysteries, its size, its apparent random chaos kept in time by an invisible Conductor, the world beyond our limited horizon reflects God in all His might and power and otherness.

The Bible's narrative picks up on the imagery too, making more than fifty references to the stars across the two testaments. We first read of God as the Creator of the planets: "God made two great lights—the greater light to govern the day and the lesser light to govern the night. He also made the stars" (Gen. 1:16).

This view of God as Author of cosmic creation is part of common understanding. Job brushed aside the impatient foolishness of his so-called friends, declaring, "He shakes the earth from its place and makes its pillars tremble. He speaks to the sun and it does not shine; he seals off the light of the stars. He alone stretches out the heavens and treads on the waves of the sea" (Job 9:6–8).

When God finally broke the silence that has hung over Job, He

> "Few things help an individual more than to place responsibility upon him, and to let him know that you trust him."
> —Booker T. Washington

revealed another side of His character. The Almighty took a more muscular approach, demanding that Job stand up to hear the charge: "Where were you when I laid the earth's foundation? Tell me, if you understand. Who marked off its dimensions? Surely you know! Who stretched a measuring line across it? On what were its footings set, or who laid its cornerstone—while the morning stars sang together and all the angels shouted for joy?" (Job 38:4–7)

The stars can offer no hiding place, as the prophet Obadiah found out as many as 2,800 years ago: "'Though you soar like the eagle and make your nest among the stars, from there I will bring you down,' declares the Lord" (Obad. 4).

While the Bible starts by exploring the care that God lavished upon

His creation, by the end the tone shifts significantly. Take a look at the book of Revelation—the scenes surrounding the apocalypse are overwhelming.

"I watched as he opened the sixth seal. There was a great earthquake. The sun turned black like sackcloth made of goat hair, the whole moon turned blood red, and the stars in the sky fell to earth, as figs drop from a fig tree when shaken by a strong wind. The sky receded like a scroll, rolling up, and every mountain and island was removed from its place" (Rev. 6:12–14).

In spite of the power ...

So the stars are powerful. Their very mass creates a gravity that we find almost impossible to escape. To God, however, these balls of liquid or gas are all subject to His even greater force. He has created, and He can extinguish. And despite all this, despite our infinitesimally insignificant size, despite the fact that we are dwarfed by forces too large to measure, we choose to leave God behind. We marvel at the gravity of the planets, yet walk away from the pull of our Creator. We are awed at the possibilities presented by black holes, yet find God's escape velocity an almost unnoticeable force. We resist God's gravity.

I resist God's gravity. Instead of giving in to the established order of things, instead of allowing my priorities and my agenda to be molded and shaped by God's passions, I choose to live in a world of my own creation, to rule over a planet defined by whatever shouts loudest in my life. Not a real planet, you understand, but a virtual one held in place by a culture that keeps me safe

WE MARVEL AT THE GRAVITY OF THE PLANETS, YET WALK AWAY FROM THE PULL OF OUR CREATOR.

from things that I'd rather not face. Like poverty. Like hunger. Like images of starving children using their last breath to plea for help. My personal planet lets me change the channel quickly and grab another treat from the fridge.

And here's what I hate about the personal planet: my faith says it shouldn't be there at all. My beliefs tell me that it's not right that all sixty million of us in the United Kingdom have access to clean drinking water while three-quarters of those in Ethiopia don't.[3] I know there's something wrong when one in three children in the United Kingdom live in poverty.[4] It can't be right when the doorway of my second-favorite junk-food retailer is the bed of choice for so many homeless.

Of course, I don't like this planet I have created, and I'm constantly trying to work up the escape velocity to leave it behind. What helps most is joining the dots between the past and the present. A couple of millennia ago, Jesus said, "A man's life does not consist in the abundance of his possessions" (Luke 12:15, NIV). I need to constantly ask if my life reflects this belief: Am I living it out when I'm stuffing my face with food I've no room for? Am I proof of its reality when I'm dreaming about the next must-have toy that I want so badly? Does my integrity look a little thin when my lifestyle fails to match up to my worship?

And this is where it all gets vital. If I'm really going to sing those songs, to tell God of my devotion and desire to be one of those living sacrifices, then I'd better not get too cozy on my personal planet. Because if I do, I'll end up like the worshipers that God reprimanded through the prophet Isaiah.

There they were, doing what they were convinced was all the right stuff—praying, fasting, and worshiping—but God didn't seem to be listening. "'Why have we fasted,' they say, 'and you have not seen it?

Why have we humbled ourselves, and you have not noticed?'" (Isa. 58:3)

Finally, they got their answer.

First, God questioned their integrity, declaring that their words just didn't match their lifestyle: "On the day of your fasting, you do as you please and exploit all your workers. Your fasting ends in quarreling and strife, and in striking each other with wicked fists. You cannot fast as you do today and expect your voice to be heard on high" (Isa. 58:3–4).

We need to check ourselves out, too. Does the way we shop, the way we dress, and the way we bank contribute to or combat the injustice we sing about? Which screams loudest to God, my words or my actions?

> **Proverbs 28:5**
> Evildoers do not understand what is right, but those who seek the Lord understand it fully.

Actions really do speak louder, more than any heartfelt song. He made it clear precisely what He was after when He addressed the Israelites: "Is not this the kind of fasting I have chosen: to loose the chains of injustice and untie the cords of the yoke, to set the oppressed free and break every yoke? Is it not to share your food with the hungry and to provide the poor wanderer with shelter—when you see the naked, to clothe them and not to turn away from your own flesh and blood?" (Isa. 58:6–7)

Without the action—the practical acts of kindness and mercy—we settle back beneath the gray skies of our limited horizons. Our words stay there with us.

Finally, the words given to Isaiah reveal the closeness of the relationship between our worship of God and our lifestyle. What God wants from us is a lifelong commitment to worship Him and, in doing so, to love others. He wants more than the promising words; He wants to actually see it all put into action. God wants us to step out of the bubble, to break free from the surface of selfish values, and to start living for something other than our own satisfaction. He wants us to live beyond our own wish lists. He tells us, "If you spend yourselves in behalf of the hungry and satisfy the needs of the oppressed, then your light will rise in the darkness, and your night will become like the noonday ... you will be called Repairer of Broken Walls, Restorer of Streets with Dwellings" (Isa. 58:10, 12).

On the surface of my personal planet it's all about me: my wants, my needs, my aims and ambitions. Beyond the atmosphere it's all about Him: His desire for an army of people who choose worship that is simple, plain, and effective because it is fair, right, impartial, honest, honorable, righteous, moral, and truthful. Outside the planet's pull, you can hear the sounds and see the sights of a type of worship that makes a difference. Away from the planet, the air is cleaner. And I've heard the view from there is pretty good, too.

How do we move on from here?

So what do we do about all this? How do we get our heads around the fact that we have been handed a mandate to assume responsibility for dispensing human justice? How do we allow ourselves to be taken in by God's gravity? How do we break out of our self-made gravities that keep us cozy and calm and wanting just one more bite of the pie before we die? We need a shift in perspective. Not a major one, perhaps, but a shift nevertheless. We need to locate the source of the escape velocity that propels us away from God's gravity. We need to find what it is that allows us to sit back and flip the channel on compassion and responsibility whenever the subjects come up.

HOW DO WE BREAK OUT OF OUR SELF-MADE GRAVITIES THAT KEEP US COZY AND CALM AND WANTING JUST ONE MORE BITE OF THE PIE BEFORE WE DIE?

Of course, submitting to God's gravity may sound like a truly horrific prospect, one every bit as bad as the idea of crossing the event horizon of a black hole. Clever people who write things on the Internet inform me that the experience wouldn't be quite as pleasantly trippy as Hollywood might have us believe. Apparently, if we fell feet-first, our bodies would end up looking something like an infinitely long bit of fusilli pasta. The gravitational pull would be much stronger on the feet than on the head, and time would slow down.[5] Actually, some other Internet guru suggested that the first body part to cross the event horizon would effectively be chopped off—stretched for eternity or severed in an instant. Neither seems that much fun.

Yet God's gravity is different. On one level it seems weaker than the black hole's, allowing us to escape at any point—yet it has more power than any force known to man. And unlike the stuff that surrounds the planets, God's gravity is easy to see. It was there on the cross, surrounding the battered flesh that had been hung, tortured, brutalized, all for Christ's compassion for a wayward people. You can see it in the lives of the apostles, who handed over their lives for a greater destiny, embracing the suffering that was the inevitable consequence of their dedication to justice and service. It was heavy in the air when William Wilberforce fought the forces of slavery, when

Martin Luther King called for equality, when Nelson Mandela chose peace. And it was there when you last gave a thought for someone other than yourself. When you last gave a little of your time, your energy, or your resources to someone who needed them more than you, God's gravity was on you. When you last made a decision not to buy into the myth that self-esteem can be boosted by material possessions, God's gravity pulled you a little closer. When you last remembered the importance of obedience and sacrifice, that was God's gravity at work. We need more of it, all of us, every day.

CHILDREN AT WAR

....

Charles fidgets while he talks, playing with hem of his trousers and the edge of the mattress he is sitting on. His story begins seven years ago, when he was eight years old, and as he talks, it's clear why his fingers reach out for something else to focus on.

Charles was a child soldier. While visiting his grandmother, he was abducted and forced to fight for the Lord's Resistance Army (LRA), Uganda's lawless rebels. During his time as a captive he was shot in the leg and lower back. He was forced to act against his will. He thinks he killed three people.

"I killed two with a stick. One I shot with a gun," he says.

He was beaten regularly, sometimes with a machete. Once, he was whipped two hundred times because he had left a bomb behind.

As he talks, it's hard to even begin to understand the impact his experiences must have had on him. The LRA rebels rule their child soldiers by fear, forcing them to commit acts that will haunt them for years. Charles was no exception.

"To stop me from escaping, they abducted someone for me to kill. I had to kill that person using a stick. I just beat him to death with a stick."

Charles' experiences, sadly, are not unique. It is estimated that 28,500 Ugandan children have been abducted since 1985, and while not all have been forced to fight, their experiences leave scars that may never vanish.

Doreen, like Charles, is fifteen years old. She too was abducted by the LRA, although her imprisonment lasted only eight months. Her story, however, is horrific. She experienced things no one should ever have to face, let alone a child. She was beaten, raped, and forced to kill her own brother. Traumatized by her experiences, she became ill and rapidly lost weight.

Far away from the innocent plastic guns of our playground, child soldiers are a shocking reality. More than 300,000 children—some as young as eight—are exploited in armed conflict in more than thirty countries around the world.[6]

"I got rashes and boils on my body," she explains. "When they saw this, they started saying that I was a wizard and that I should be killed."

Despite her illness, Doreen was forced to carry weapons across the border from Sudan. She knows the names of the weapons well—HPD9, rocket-propelled grenades, PK guns—too well for a girl her age.

Doreen was eventually helped by the Ugandan government soldiers (UPDF) after they attacked the LRA soldiers that had abducted her.

"The UPDF found us and started firing at us. I crawled away and hid under some trees," Doreen says. "I couldn't walk because I was sick, but the rebels came back and found me. They accused me of collaborating with the UPDF and beat me until I was unconscious. They left me there, thinking that I had died."

It is shocking to hear these stories and know that there are thousands more waiting to be told. Yet it is even more disturbing to know that Uganda prides itself on being an African success story. It prefers to tell people about debt relief, HIV/AIDS prevention, and exotic tourism rather than to reveal the truth about the troubled northern region of the country. After all, child soldiers and lawless rebels don't make for good headlines.

The truth is that many Ugandans feel that their government is not protecting them. People are so afraid of the LRA that every night, some forty-five thousand women and children leave their homes and head for the relative safety of nearby towns.

These night commuters face a walk of up to six miles. If they are lucky, they may be able to find a bit of floor space on the grounds of the hospital. If not, they have to make do with the streets or truck stops, at the mercy of the weather.

Jackline is six months pregnant but brings her two young children with her every night.

"The children struggle with the walk. They are too small for such distances," she says. "When it rains, we don't have shelter. It just rains on us. We can't sleep, so we stand until it stops. But I am trying to run away from the LRA, and I feel safer when I am here because there are many people around us."

> Over the last decade, it is estimated that more than two million children have died as a direct result of armed conflict. At least six million children have been seriously injured or permanently disabled. Meanwhile, between eight and ten thousand continue to be killed or maimed by landmines each year.[7]

Like 90 percent of the population, Jackline lives in a camp created by the Ugandan government. They are supposed to be "safe zones," but in recent weeks, camp attacks have left eighty dead and two hundred huts destroyed. It is little wonder that they choose to get out at night.

Those who are fortunate find themselves at Noah's Ark, a project that offers safety and security for many children. There they can play volleyball or football, or do homework before sleeping in safety.

The war in Uganda is nearly two decades old. Some accuse the government of allowing it to continue; others blame the international community for failing to step in. Yet others point out the horribly twisted difficulties of a war where the "enemy" is one's own children. Whatever the answer to Uganda's problems, it is clear that the work of Noah's Ark is vital if those like Charles and Doreen are to pick up their lives again.

CHAPTER THREE

Gravity's Consequence

The Bible has plenty to say about the forces that are at work upon our lives. Through illustration, parable, metaphor, and direct example, its pages explore and expound upon some essential themes. People with bigger brains than mine can draw out all manner of wonderful interpretations, seeing anything from sex and gardening to the restoration of true relationship between Creator and created. Maybe this says more about my own issues than it does about my insight, but the Bible just seems to scream out a clear and constant message: the story of the human race has been plagued by our struggles with ego.

From the story in the garden to the scenes on the way to the cross, mankind places himself at the center of the universe, forcing God into second place. We have an ability to ignore the bigger picture and focus our attention so narrowly on our own lives and its mixed bag of wants, hurts, needs, desires, and fears that we spectacularly manage to miss the point of life again and again. There's Peter slashing and dashing in the Garden of Gethsemane; Samson seducing and murdering his way around his home region; Noah lying splayed, naked, and drunk on home brew after the flood; or David taking a little break from kingly duties to spy on naked babes from the palace roof. Mankind has a habit of messing up by looking down.

Yet while these four individuals undoubtedly messed up, their failures are put in context of their relationship with a loving, forgiving, intimate God. To really see what the Bible has to say about the art of escaping God's gravity, we need to take a look at those who viewed the Lord as irrelevant, unfamiliar, or just plain offensive. And there are plenty of them, particularly the ones with power.

Like Pharaoh. Due to some difficulties with the climate, Abraham (then called Abram) and his wife, Sarah (then known as Sarai), chose to escape severe famine and head to Egypt. Genesis 12 describes Abram's anxiety about the prospect of the Egyptians taking a liking to his fine lady and his assumption that because she was so hot, they were bound to murder him once they found out the two were married. So he suggested that they pose as brother and sister. Of course by then, the whole thing was firmly bolted onto the tracks of tragedy, and anyone could see the imminent disaster looming— anyone, that is, except Abram, who continued to perpetuate this "traveling sibling" routine once they arrived.

He was right, too. The Egyptians saw Sarai, liked her, and told Pharaoh all about her. He, in turn, treated Abram well, giving him plenty of material possessions to sweeten him up for what we assume is the inevitable invitation for Sarai to take her place in the ruler's harem. Then it all went wrong:

> But the Lord inflicted serious diseases on Pharaoh and
> his household because of Abram's wife Sarai. So Pharaoh
> summoned Abram. "What have you done to me?" he said.
> "Why didn't you tell me she was your wife? Why did you
> say, 'She is my sister,' so that I took her to be my wife? Now
> then, here is your wife. Take her and go!" Then Pharaoh gave
> orders about Abram to his men, and they sent him on his
> way, with his wife and everything he had. (Gen. 12:17–20)

Pharaoh was perhaps understandably annoyed. Yet why did he allow them to leave? It seems that the material wealth Abram reaped was not so much an indication that God approved of his half-truth (for she was in fact his half-sister—see Gen. 20:12), but rather a question of grace. After all, Abram was the faithful follower to whom God had promised offspring as numerous as the stars. The presence of such a man could have made a profound impact upon the ruler, but instead he chose to sulk as his latest favorite object of lust was removed from his grasp.

The result?
An antipathy toward Abram's descendants that passed from Pharaoh to Pharaoh.

> **Proverbs 29:4**
> By justice a king gives a country stability, but those who are greedy for bribes tear it down.

By the time we get to Exodus 1, the Egyptian rulers are past masters at oppressing the Israelites. The situation had become so bad that the pattern repeated once more. With Moses as the leader of God's people this time, more plagues were handed out on the Egyptian people. Eventually this Pharaoh gave in and told Moses that the Israelites could head off into the sunset—but without their livestock or possessions. No deal, said Moses. Without livestock, their chances of either surviving or worshiping God were as good as worthless.

"But the Lord hardened Pharaoh's heart, and he was not willing to let them go. Pharaoh said to Moses, 'Get out of my sight! Make sure you do not appear before me again! The day you see my face you will die.' 'Just as you say,' Moses replied. 'I will never appear before you again'" (Exod. 10:27–29).

Again, a man chose to place his own appetite ahead of bigger concerns. Plagues of blood, frogs, gnats, flies, disease, boils, hail, locusts, and darkness had all failed to shake Pharaoh. His predecessor had been riled by the loss of an object of his sexual fantasy, and Moses' opponent simply refused to countenance the idea of life without an easily oppressible, readily available supply of slave labor.

Years later, the power of the groin was still on show in the life of Herod. Matthew 14 tells us how the king of Galilee and Peraea got a little hot under the collar when John the Baptist started to criticize his actions. Herod had divorced his first wife to marry Herodias, wife of his half-brother Herod Philip.

"John had been saying to him: 'It is not lawful for you to have her.' Herod wanted to kill John, but he was afraid of the people, because they considered him a prophet" (Matt. 14:4–5).

The union ruined Herod, not to mention John. Herod's initial father-in-law fought the wayward king and destroyed one of Herod's armies in the process. Yet it is the image of John's head, severed and served on a plate, that endures today, the symbol of the extent to which one man went simply to satisfy his sexual desires.

Earlier, much earlier, there were other rulers whose refusal to have their authority challenged resulted in further oppression, destruction, and sin. Look at the death of Zechariah, son of Jehoiada the priest. He criticized the current trend of abandoning the worship of God. The result was swift: "But they plotted against him, and by order of the king they stoned him to death in the courtyard of the Lord's temple. King Joash did not remember the kindness Zechariah's father Jehoiada had shown him but killed his son, who said as he lay dying, 'May the Lord see this and call you to account'" (2 Chron. 24:21–22).

A little earlier on, the plot revolved around familiar themes; the prophet Hanani got a little too close for comfort to Asa, king of Judah:

Because you relied on the king of Aram and not on the
Lord your God, the army of the king of Aram has escaped
from your hand. Were not the Cushites and Libyans a
mighty army with great numbers of chariots and horsemen?
Yet when you relied on the Lord, he delivered them into
your hand. For the eyes of the Lord range throughout the
earth to strengthen those whose hearts are fully committed
to him. You have done a foolish thing, and from now on you
will be at war. (2 Chron. 16:7–9)

Asa didn't like hearing this. So he got angry, slammed Hanani in
prison, tortured him, and did more of the same to others. Asa went
down in history for, among other things, being the first ruler to
mistreat a prophet for simply doing his job. Offended at the slight to
his ego, bruised by the truth that he had stopped relying on God and
started depending on his own resources and feeding his own appetite,
Asa joined the ranks of the Pharaohs, Herod, and Joash. These men of
power made their world revolve around themselves, refusing to allow
God's wider perspective to challenge or redirect.

In 2 Chronicles 26 we read about Uzziah, freshly intoxicated by
political power. Nothing was off limits, not even the temple. Strolling
in, he decided to get a little incense burning, believing that anything
a priest could do, he could easily do too. Confronted by eighty angry
clerics who caught him in the act, Uzziah reacted in a fashion typical
of the self-obsession that plagues us still:

Uzziah, who had a censer in his hand ready to burn incense,
became angry. While he was raging at the priests in their
presence before the incense altar in the Lord's temple,
leprosy broke out on his forehead. When Azariah the chief
priest and all the other priests looked at him, they saw that
he had leprosy on his forehead, so they hurried him out.
Indeed, he himself was eager to leave, because the Lord

had afflicted him. King Uzziah had leprosy until the day he died. He lived in a separate house—leprous, and excluded from the temple of the Lord. Jotham his son had charge of the palace and governed the people of the land. (2 Chron. 26:19–21)

The book of Numbers adds to the theme, with the story of Balak getting mightily annoyed at the way God's plan deviated from his own. "I summoned you to curse my enemies ... but you have blessed them these three times. Now leave at once and go home!" (Num. 24:10–11)

The sulking Balak is joined by Ahab, one of the early kings of Israel. Considering the merits of a military campaign—one that would ultimately claim his life—he sought confirmation from the prophets of his decision to attack. Four hundred agreed, yet Ahab resisted hearing the opinion of Micaiah, son of Imlah. "I hate him because he never prophesies anything good about me" (1 Kings 22:8). At least he was honest, I suppose. Micaiah told the truth, got sent to prison for it, and presumably resisted the urge to say "I told you so" when he heard of Ahab's death at Ramoth Gilead.

Naaman sulked, too. A fine warrior and man of influence, he became troubled when he was struck with leprosy. He journeyed to Elisha's house, hoping the prophet might be able to cure him. Yet when Elisha merely advised him to go and wash seven times in the Jordan River, Naaman was offended.

"But Naaman went away angry and said, 'I thought that he would surely come out to me and stand and call on the name of the Lord his God, wave his hand over the spot and cure me of my leprosy'" (2 Kings 5:11).

God does not work the way we want Him to. It is a fact—an

uncomfortable one, perhaps, but a fact nevertheless—that our part of the deal boils down to loving and serving God. It's a great deal, one with some fine fringe benefits, but if we see ourselves as existing merely to have our own needs, wants, and desires met, we're going to end up disappointed.

The consequences of the me-first agenda: part one (us)

Looking back over the list of biblical non-believers who were offended by God, we can see a couple of deeper threads joining them together. All were guilty of creating their own personal planets, of refusing to give in to God's gravity, but I wonder if they divide down even further. The two Pharaohs and Herod make for a clear threesome. Each pursued the satisfaction of his own appetite, whether for sexual gratification or a lifestyle of luxury. None seemed too concerned with the consequences of his actions. Pharaoh allowed Abraham to keep his wealth but appeared indifferent to the potential hardship he was inflicting on the couple seeking refuge in Egypt. Similarly, his later successor spared no thought for the suffering of the Israelites and felt no remorse for his oppression. If Herod agonized at all over his decision to behead John, it was made easier by the sight of Salome's dance.

Furthermore, they were all concerned with the aspect of public embarrassment: both Pharaohs

GOD DOES NOT WORK THE WAY WE WANT HIM TO.

suffered plagues for their troubles, and Herod was unwilling to lose face in front of his guests when Herodias asked for John's head. So it seems that these flawed rulers are joined by common threads: the desire to gratify human desire and the distinct dislike of losing face in public.

Joash, Asa, and Uzziah all strayed from God. They all decided that He was no longer necessary to their success and chose to wander away from obedience. Joash opted to forget the kindness of Zechariah's father Jehoiada; Asa moved on from his earlier reliance on God; and Uzziah, a boy-king at sixteen, gradually lost momentum. At first "he did what was right in the eyes of the Lord" (2 Chron. 26:4). Later he served himself. These three illustrate our own capacity to believe that we can outgrow God, that we can move on from a position of service and have things our own way instead.

Percentage of those between the ages of eighteen and twenty-nine who think they have a very good chance of achieving "the good life":

1978: 41%
1993: 21%[1]

And then there are Balak, Ahab, and Naaman, three sorry specimens who simply stamped their feet because God chose to do things differently than how they had hoped. Their assumptions about the Lord's will were based on their own self-obsessed ideals. Balak wanted God to kill, Ahab wanted one more victory, and Naaman simply was not used to being treated with anything less than the highest degree of respect. For these men, the prospect of being humbled by God was a distinctly uncomfortable process.

You know what's coming next. The threads that unite these three groups of biblical personal planet-dwellers can be traced all the way up to our door, too. We resist God, pull back from orbit in favor of making our own worlds, of living life according to our own agendas.

Like the Pharaohs and Herod, we allow our lives to revolve around our appetites, gorging ourselves on the so-called treats that give us such a fleeting high. We make this world about what we can get, what we can consume, what we can taste—all the time reducing its size. We make our world too small, our horizons too limited, our sun too pale. The materialist on his deathbed knows this; his life's pursuit of gain and greed is finally revealed as nothing but a waste.

We share the temptations of Joash and Asa and Uzziah, too. We want a world that is safe, where we are in control, not the almighty Creator, the One we cannot pin down, box in, or predict. We place ourselves on the throne and rely on ourselves alone. We take the reins in the hope that life will work out a little better if we can control it. Yet this control is a mirage, at best an ice sculpture on a summer's dawn. Can we control our lives? Can we really leave God out?

And then there's the temptation that vanity offers. Life's guiding star becomes our own reputation. Balak, Ahab, and Naaman all struggled to humble themselves—an essential part of relationship with God. The cross shows us this truth in bold. Where was the dignity in an undeserved flogging, a criminal's death, a borrowed grave? John stumbled from behind the bars of his prison cell, asking if Jesus really was the One they had all been waiting for. He knew the answer better than any man on earth, yet Jesus' reply cleared away any doubt: "Blessed is the man who does not fall away on account of me" (Matt. 11:6, NIV). It may not run according to our plan, but God's gravity demands that we take the small steps required, that we act out of obedience instead of arrogance.

The consequences of the me-first agenda: part two (them)

We're good at resisting God's gravity. We indulge, ignore, and preen ourselves out of His orbit. Yet does the story end there? Is all that matters the fact that we get a little selfish from time to time and really ought to think about God a little more? Sadly, no. This whole idea of living in the isolation of our own personal planet gives a false sense of security, allowing us to pretend for a minute that our actions occur without consequence to others. This is untrue and introduces just one more layer to be scraped away from the stories of our biblical failure—a layer that reveals the bigger picture. Most of these men contributed in some way to the suffering of others. Whether it was slavery, murder, torture, imprisonment, or oppression, these individuals with influence did not act in a vacuum. Their actions affected others, just like ours do.

But Naaman was different. He knew he had been self-obsessed and vain, and accepted the healing delivered through Elisha's advice. Yet the story did not end there. Elisha's servant Gehazi wondered if they should have suggested that Naaman give a little cash as a token of his gratitude. Elisha sent Gehazi to collect the gift, and the freshly healed and humbled Naaman gladly handed over double the amount requested, an impressive two talents—125 pounds or 70 kilos—of silver. Gehazi kept the cash from Elisha, who was anything but stupid. The result for Gehazi was drastic: banishment, as well as the onset of the very leprosy from which Naaman had just been healed.

Gehazi's mistake was simple: he was greedy and dishonest and kept for himself that which had been freely given to support the work of God. Naaman came out well; Jesus even recalled his unique healing to a skeptical audience at His hometown synagogue.

What about us? Whatever we touch we have the power to use for good or bad. Just like Naaman's gift, our fingerprints are left all over the world in which we live.

It is comforting to believe that our personal planets are self-contained, that they offer us protection from the world around us and shield us from enduring or inflicting harm. Yet we are fools if we see them as anything other than fragile and flawed creations. We are misguided if we believe for one minute that our actions do not share many of the same consequences that the Pharaohs and kings faced. But we'll come to all that a little later on. For now, it's time to ask what sort of planets we make for ourselves.

MATTERS OF LIFE AND DEATH

....

Nine million people worldwide live with tuberculosis (TB). Each year, two million die from the disease, while another staggering two billion carry the bacterium in their bodies. But these aren't just numbers—these are real people with real lives.

JANHJO

Janhjo was twenty-one when she got married. For the first year of marriage, she was unable to work, cook, or—more importantly, from her in-laws' point of view—provide grandchildren. Not only does tuberculosis threaten her health, it threatens her place within society, even within her own family.

After seeing her grandmother die recently from the sickness, Janhjo is desperate to get well. She spent all her money on two weeks' worth of treatment from a local doctor. This did not help. She has also traveled ten miles to a clinic that she heard offered free eight-month supplies of drugs.

SANGITA

At sixty, Kheair has already buried two of his eight children, slain by a strain of tuberculosis that was resistant to treatment. Now two more have caught it—Sangita, eighteen, and her twenty-four-year-old brother, Santosh, who is responding well to the treatment. Sangita has been given spiritual and medical support by a project paramedic, Imrose. But, he explains, the news is not good: "Sangita seems to be resistant. She has had three courses and three failures. She will die from tuberculosis. She is young and unmarried, and may die within the year."

[Sadly, Imrose was right. Sangita died from tuberculosis shortly before this book went to print. Our prayers are with her family. Will our actions be there to support the others living with this disease?]

MEJAHR

Mejahr is ill. She has a cough, fever, and fatigue, and has lost her appetite. These classic signs point unmistakably to tuberculosis. With no money for transportation, her family can't get her to a clinic for testing. Her grandfather, Soomar, walked more than seven miles with her to get the tests done.

Without the clinic, the drugs would be far too expensive. Death would be inevitable. Soomar knows how important the clinic is.

"My wife caught TB and we spent money to treat it, but she died. People told us about this clinic. The treatment here is free. I pray for my granddaughter to get well."

VEERO

Landless, poor, and ill, thirty-year-old Veero is in a dangerous situation.

"I feel like I have a broken body—broken with weakness," he says. "Before TB I could plant a quarter of an acre with chili seedlings. With TB, I can only plant one-sixteenth of an acre—a quarter of what I could plant before."

He and his son have been infected for three months. The family lives hand to mouth, scraping together just enough food to survive. In order to go to the hospital they must borrow money from the landowner, but it often goes beyond the limits of the crops they raise to pay him back.

BHALLA

At fifty-two, tuberculosis-infected Bhalla has hope. He began treatment two months ago and visits the Bodel Farm Christian Tuberculosis Control Clinic regularly.

"I live in Karimabad, which is almost four miles from the clinic," he explains. "My landowner brought me on his motorcycle because I am one of his tenant workers. I have been too weak to work since getting TB, so my three sons work to provide money. TB has given me breathing problems and a cough and made me very weak. I have been on the medication for two months."

KAMLESH

Kamlesh, safe in the arms of his devoted grandmother, is one-and-a-half years old. But he is ill.

"He's become weak and has had symptoms of TB for several months," his grandmother explains. "His mother had TB. She was successfully treated here at the Christian TB center in Kunri, and is now well."

Poor families like Kamlesh's often sleep in one room. Tuberculosis spreads in warm, airless places, so when one member catches it, the entire family is often at risk. By treating one person, the clinic could prevent many more from catching it.

IMROSE

Imrose cares for more than just his patients' physical health.

"Before my work, I pray every day. I pray with my workers for my patients," he says.

As chief paramedic in the Diocese of Hyderabad Tuberculosis Control Program in Pakistan, Imrose is a true man of vision. He knows the disease can be eradicated. He has seen the power the drugs have, when taken correctly, to kill the disease. Thanks to the support of Christians around the world, his clinics offer free drugs.

"At least three patients die each month because they took drugs from a private doctor and don't have the money to finish the course. Private treatment is very expensive, and patients cannot afford eight months' worth."

Inspired by Jesus' example of reaching out to a leper in Matthew 8:1–4, Imrose and his team are engaged in a battle to stop tuberculosis in Pakistan.

....

TUBERCULOSIS: FACTS

Over the next twelve months, almost 1.7 million people will die simply because they've been too close to someone breathing out the deadly disease. It's as simple, as innocent, as shocking as that. Tuberculosis spreads with the ease of a common cold.

What is truly shocking is that we can easily treat it. With a full course of drugs, the disease will die—and the patient will not. If the drugs are unavailable or too expensive, or if the treatment is not carried out to the end, death is the overwhelming outcome—as it was for Sangita. All from a cough. All from a sneeze. All from being too close to the wrong person at the wrong time.

We live in a world where we have real power. We have money. We have a voice. We have knowledge. We know that tuberculosis is entirely preventable, yet it remains one of the biggest killers in the world today.

The story here is not just about these individuals. It's also about you and me. So we might have the scars to prove our vaccination against the disease— but does that mean we are to have no more to do with it? Have our hearts and minds been neutralized from the effects of this devastating killer?

It wasn't always like this. We wealthy Westerners were not always so carefree. Tuberculosis was a global threat, from the first civilizations, until fairly recently. In 1815 it claimed one in four deaths in England. Eventually, in 1880, people figured out that the disease was contagious and made moves to stop it from spreading. Spitting in public was banned, and the poor who were infected were carted off to a sanatorium—part hospital, part prison. Three-quarters of the people that entered the sanatoria were dead within five years. French scientists found a vaccination in 1921, but it took another twenty years before British, American, or German governments started handing out the treatment.

Since then, scientists have developed antibiotics that can cure a patient, and pasteurization now stops the spread of tuberculosis from cows to humans through milk. In fact, if it hadn't been for lapses in public health and the rise of stronger, drug-resistant strains of the disease in the 1980s, many thought the disease would never trouble the West again. But with the number of reported cases rising in the United Kingdom and as many as twenty thousand cases in New York throughout the 1980s, it seems that we are far from being completely safe. In fact, in 1993 the World Health Organization declared a global health emergency in response to the disease. Ten years later, things had gotten even worse. By experimenting with genes, researchers accidentally created a more lethal and rapidly reproducing strain.

Tuberculosis affects the poor far more than the wealthy. Those suffering today in London or New York are the poor—those who cannot afford adequate shelter, who do not have access to drug treatments. Around the rest of the world, the disease is less selective. Two billion people carry it right now, and while only 10 percent of those infected will go on to develop the disease, the ones who do and cannot access treatment will stand just a 50 percent chance of surviving.

"Poor people are most at risk," explains Imrose. "They live in small homes with four or five family members. If one has TB, they will cough and others will get it."

Looking at the statistics, the twenty countries with the highest rates of tuberculosis all happen to be poor. The reality is that most of the nine million people who catch the sickness have little money to fight the disease.

"Patients die each month because they take drugs from a private doctor and don't have the money to finish the course," explains Imrose.

Each pill costs six rupees (slightly more than seven pence or twelve cents). Treatment requires four pills a day, totaling nearly 170 rupees a week ($3.77). The average weekly wage for a worker in Pakistan is five hundred rupees. So for a family already living hand to mouth, this means a third of their wages must be spent on medication.

World leaders know that tuberculosis is curable, and they know how vital it is to tackle the problem. But sadly, they are dragging their heels. With the effective treatment program DOTS (Directly Observed Therapy Short-course) in place, as many as 95 percent of those with the disease in the poorest countries could be cured. DOTS is the internationally recommended control strategy. It sets standards for effective treatment, including uninterrupted supplies of drugs and assisted observation to ensure that patients do not miss out on any treatment. A six-month supply of drugs under the DOTS strategy costs as little as $10.13 per patient in some parts of the world.

> Tuberculosis is preventable. Not just partially preventable, but wholly so. If patients do not take their full course of drugs—and there are many reasons why this can happen—drug-resistant strains of the disease emerge.

Tuberculosis is treatable, but the treatment is still being kept from those in need. Tuberculosis is preventable, but people still die. Tuberculosis is curable, but another child in Africa will die before you finish reading this paragraph. In a world where money and popular opinion can move mountains, are we sure there is nothing we can do to halt its savage progress?

CHAPTER 4

Our World
Is Too Small

So there was this man named Job. According to the story he was blameless and upright, feared God, and did whatever he could to resist evil. He was a seriously good guy in the eyes of God. And he was rich. Really rich. He had it all—the big family and the even bigger business. With seven thousand sheep to his name, three thousand camels, five hundred oxen, five hundred donkeys, and a whole load of servants, it's hardly surprising that he was also known as "the greatest man among all the people of the East" (Job 1:3).

For those of us surrounded by the treats of wealth, it is tempting to consider that Job's greatness of character and greatness of bank balance were in some way linked. His wealth can easily sound like the reason for his greatness, rather than a consequence of it. After all, isn't that precisely the way we handle things around here? Those of us who have the potential to increase our earnings will find ourselves raking in the money and the power and the influence. We'll work our way to greatness, given the right start and circumstances.

I wonder how Job's story would sound to us if we had nothing; I wonder if we'd be impressed if we came from a different background. I don't mean if we lost our wealth and ended up destitute with our noses pressed up against the glass of our privileged Western lifestyle—

I mean if we had never known anything other than a hand-to-mouth existence. Would we deduce a different meaning if we knew personally the frailty of the string by which our life dangled? What if we depended on the land and had been thrown into chaos, real poverty, and even death by the unpredictability of the seasons? I think we'd see Job differently.

Here in the affluent West we rate material wealth highly, yet in the Church we know that this isn't quite right. Whether it's our faith or our conscience or our understanding of global economics, we know that our possessions do not define us or underpin our self-worth, that our Visa card is not the provider of anything but perhaps a fleeting high. We know that, don't we?

The truth is that we struggle. We struggle to break free of the influence of money and possessions and all the stuff that twinkles and glitters and tells us to grab it, all the stuff that convinces us that we have to have it right now. A part of our brain may know the truth, may see the bigger picture and acknowledge that all of this shuffling around the trough of consumer goods won't give us lasting, eternal peace, but at times it feels as if we are almost powerless to resist.

If we believe in God, if we believe in His existence and omnipotence, then we believe in His authorship and ultimate ownership of all things. If we believe in His Son's life, death, and resurrection, then we believe in the unimportance of physical wealth, compared to the value of relationship with God. But believing in the big picture and translating it to the daily script of our lives are two different things altogether. I believe in God's power and values, yet a quick look at the history tab of my Internet browser tells another story. There you'll see that I've idly flicked over flights and cars and books and computers during the last thirty-six hours, contemplating some vague idea of purchase. I've even been looking into the prospect of buying some chickens, for heaven's sake. I many not have actually bought anything, but the thought of owning these things is a recreational pursuit that I do almost without thinking.

Not that the Internet is wrong, or that browsing or purchasing is bad. But do you see the point? I believe in the big picture; I believe that Job's greatness was bound up in his service to God; I believe in God's gravity—yet I get so easily distracted by trivial things. I make my world too small. I declare that God owns it all, yet I act with all the manic possessiveness of a sleep-deprived toddler at a Christmas party.

Which reminds me of my daughter, Evie. She's uniquely funny and bright and remarkable and was able to look out of the window one morning when she was almost three and say, "It's raining and it's sunny. That's a paradox." But when it comes to sharing her toys, she changes. Instead of being this wide-eyed girl, the sort who stares at neon signs at night and says, "Daddy, I'm just thinking about how beautiful the world is," her universe begins and ends with what she can possess. With guests coming to stay this weekend, the tension's already in the air, building up to the highly probable breakdown of friendship

I DECLARE THAT GOD OWNS IT ALL, YET I ACT WITH ALL THE MANIC POSSESSIVENESS OF A SLEEP-DEPRIVED TODDLER AT A CHRISTMAS PARTY.

and goodwill. There will come a point when she, surrounded by a whole stack of toys and dresses and stuff—none of which she gained through anything other than the generosity of others—will lose it. She'll be desperate not to let go of things that she sees as her own. And all of our soft words about who bought this and who owns that will do little to overcome that deeply primal urge within her to own things.

At times like these her world is too small. In a three-year-old, this is both understandable and kind of endearing. In people her parents' age, it's simply embarrassing. But we all do it, to some extent—we all see the earth and everything in it as fair game for the stamp of human ownership. We all want stuff to be ours. It seems ridiculous when corporations try to claim ownership of words such as *virgin* and *mac*, but in our own ways we do the same. Instead of seeing all things as gifts from God, we see them as part of our own hoard.

The Bible says otherwise: "The earth is the Lord's, and everything in it," declares the psalmist (Ps. 24:1). Whatever we have has come from the Lord's hand, and the dubious status of our ownership is at best only an indirect coincidence (see 1 Chronicles 29:14). In the same way that Evie's room belongs to her, our wealth is merely in our possession for a temporary, accountable duration. God places it in our care and expects us not only to give it back at the end, but also to take care of it for this time.

This small, small world we wrestle with, this planetary mass that revolves around our desire to acquire and possess whatever glitters under our gaze, brings with it some serious consequences. Alongside the practical implications of our drive toward consumption—and we'll make time to look at that in the final chapters of this book— our spiritual development gets hamstrung by our myopic outlook, our short-sighted take on just what really counts for treasure in God's scheme of things.

Life's true treasure

When we talk about treasure, about what we value in life, we so often consider it in terms of its weight. We get seduced by the gold, the girth, or the sheer mass of it. We're locked into a very physical understanding of things, which is logical, but also unreliable. Take a look at the Bible, and it's clear that the jewels available there are not the sort you'd find on display in your nearest BMW dealership.

In what Matthew records as Jesus' final seminar with the disciples before the Passover, the air was pregnant with a sense of significance. The disciples had pointed out the temple and wondered aloud what kind of time frame Jesus had in mind with regard to the whole "end of time" thing. He told them that things would get worse first and that it would be foolish and unwise to try to predict the moment of His return.

Then He started talking about virgins. And servants burying cash. And sheep and goats sitting in front of a king. Thankfully the imagery is clear and the symbolism sharp, illustrating the importance of taking God seriously. The five virgins who carry extra oil get the thumbs up, as does the servant who invests the money placed in his charge. Those who are criticized—the five virgins who end up locked out and kept away from the bridegroom, as well as the "worthless servant" who is thrown outside "into the darkness, where there will be weeping and gnashing of teeth" (Matt. 25:30)—are vilified because of one simple, common thing: they think only of themselves. Their worlds are too small. They refuse to acknowledge the bigger picture, dwelling only upon their own needs or fears or risks of losing a reward.

We can also look at the stories another way, focusing on the rewards handed out. The five wise virgins are invited to join in the banquet, and the "good and faithful" servants are invited to "come and share" in their master's happiness (Matt. 25:21, 23). The reward is not the big cash payout, but rather the chance of relationship with the Master.

God's treasure is eternal life with Him, a relationship made possible through the death of His Son. This is the worldview worth getting into focus. Who cares about possessions when we have the opportunity to be called "good and faithful friend" by the Almighty?

The uncomfortable truth

So this is all very nice, yes? We're getting along fine right now, thinking about how God really likes it best when we choose not to stress too much about what we can earn, own, or show off as we walk away from the cash register. All we need to do is get things in better perspective and we'll be fine, right? We might even end up like Job—holy and loaded. Now that's a tasty combination.

And it would be fine to believe in all this if it weren't for one small problem: it's a lie. Not that the Bible doesn't say all this about Job and the virgins and the servants—it does—but to simply stop here is to hold back from telling the whole story.

It's all about the sheep and the goats. After Jesus was done encouraging His disciples to open their eyes and see the bigger picture, to treat every day as one that counted and not to slack in their faith, He got a little agricultural. He described God's final judgment like the separation of sheep and goats by the shepherd. They—we—will be put into one of two groups. Those on one side will be welcomed, while those on the

> "Genuine politics—even politics worthy of the name—the only politics I am willing to devote myself to—is simply a matter of serving those around us: serving the community and serving those who will come after us. Its deepest roots are moral because it is a responsibility expressed through action, to and for the whole."
>
> —Václav Havel

other will not. Instead, "they will go away to eternal punishment" (Matt. 25:46).

There should be an obvious question forming in a brain cell near you right now, one that asks something like "How do we get on the right side?" There might be an answer kicking about there too, one that goes along the lines of "If you've signed up already, you're in." And that's where it all gets a little bit tricky. You see, according to Matthew's retelling of Jesus' story, the sole criterion to spending eternity with God is this: responsibility. Did the people feed the poor, befriend the stranger, clothe the naked, help the sick, or support the oppressed? If so, they made it through. If not ... they didn't.

According to Jesus' story, what God wants is to see us looking beyond ourselves, noticing and responding to the needs of others. And not just any old set of "others"—not just the nice pretty ones who might be able to get us some kind of promotion or recognition if we treat them right—but the *other* sort of others. The least. The lost. The last. The outsiders. The outcasts. The wrong people. The sort of individuals from whom our cozy lives continually keep us insulated. They are the ones we must care for. They are the people God's gravity draws us toward.

It's strong stuff, isn't it? Does it leave you feeling a little nervous? Does it leave you with doubts about how your lifestyle matches up? It does for me. And I think that's just the way God likes us—feeling uncomfortable at the thought that this small world into which we are tempted to retreat will really do us no good at all.

What life is all about

The Bible serves up a fine blend of characters whose narrow worldviews prohibited them from focusing on anything other than their immediate desires. David went through a significantly short-sighted period—resulting in murder, adultery, and shame—as did Jonah. Then there was Samson, the flawed judge whose life story closed on the note that he killed many more when he died than when he lived (see Judges 16:30). After all his promise and potential, Samson's life and death were marked by chaos and destruction. All because he liked the buzz he got from the taste of forbidden fruits.

WE DON'T GET A GOLD WATCH AFTER FIFTY YEARS OF SERVICE OR A SET OF TERRACOTTA ESPRESSO CUPS WITH EVERY SOUL WE SAVE.

What do we learn from them? We see the seductive power of self, the potential to lose the plot over something as basic and everyday as sexual desire, apathy, or stubbornness. But we see the resolution, too—the way back from the badlands of self-centered living. Just look at Psalm 51, the words of a man whose perspective had been righted once more.

"Create in me a pure heart, O God, and renew a steadfast spirit within me. Do not cast me from your presence or take your Holy Spirit from me …You do not delight in sacrifice, or I would bring it; you do not take pleasure in burnt offerings. My sacrifice, O God, is a broken spirit; a broken and contrite heart you, God, will not despise" (Ps. 51:10–11, 16-17).

He went to the heart of the matter: what matters most is the heart. David's sin was against others, but worst of all, against God. It was the heart-issue that grieved, the sacking of power, the betrayal of the mighty Savior.

The picture becomes clear: God's gravity is about more than physics; it goes beyond the physical, to the heart. The things we can grab and buy and touch are of secondary importance to our response to God's call. That's why Jesus managed to surround Himself with such a mixed bag of disciples, people from all sectors of contemporary society.

Ours is not a faith that gets validated by trophies or rewarded by physical mementos. We don't get a gold watch after fifty years of service or a set of terracotta espresso cups with every soul we save. What we get is far more valuable, yet far less tangible: the chance to be called a good and faithful friend by the Creator of all things.

It's about the heart, about allowing God to rule over ours. That's why Jesus spent those final hours before the treadmill to the cross making it perfectly clear: we need to be ready, to take God seriously, to be after relationship with Him rather than our own desires.

God's anger management

While David's repentance reveals this valuable lesson about what God likes, there are plenty of other biblical narratives that explore the things that give God displeasure, from His anger at the destruction of the world's abundance and harmony to His frustration with the constant flip-flopping of His people between devotion and selfishness. The prophets act as divine mouthpieces on these issues, and when they get fired up, there's little doubt about what angers God.

Take Amos. He was a farmer a few miles south of Bethlehem. God gave him a vision of the future and told him to take the message to the Northern Kingdom. The people there were putting on a good show, doing some slick religious activities, but failing to fool God, who saw their hearts and the way they oppressed the poor. First Amos delivered a condemnation of all the nations that had sinned against both Him and the Israelites. Perhaps it was really crowd-pleasing stuff, and it certainly made for a nice buildup to what came next: Amos turned to his Israelite audience and pronounced God's judgment on them.

"Proclaim to the fortresses of Ashdod and to the fortresses of Egypt: 'Assemble yourselves on the mountains of Samaria; see the great unrest within her and the oppression among her people.' 'They do not know how to do right,' declares the Lord, 'who store up in their fortresses what they have plundered and looted'" (Amos 3:9–10).

The Egyptians were told about the true behavior of the Israelites, who themselves had become oppressors, much as the Egyptians had abused the Israelites in previous generations. They had become numb to the eternal truth of God, dead to the acknowledgment that their actions came with consequences. By hoarding, plundering, and oppressing, they had incurred God's wrath. So what was their fate?

"This is what the Lord says: 'As a shepherd saves from the lion's mouth only two leg bones or a piece of an ear, so will the Israelites be saved, those who sit in Samaria on the edge of their beds and in Damascus on their couches'" (Amos 3:12).

At first glance this bit about bones being saved might seem optimistic—I mean, at least there was going to be something left— but it's nothing of the sort. If a shepherd brought back a few sheep bones after an attack from a wild animal, he was simply covering himself. The bones were proof that the sheep had been entirely destroyed—that there was nothing left and that it hadn't simply wandered off. So it doesn't look quite so good for those Israelites reclining in the lap of luxury, does it?

Verse 14 mentions Israel's sins, reminding us again that it was their oppression and hoarding that had run afoul of God's law. And if that wasn't clear enough, God threatened to demolish the spoils of their wayward behavior: "I will tear down the winter house along with the summer house; the houses adorned with ivory will be destroyed and the mansions will be demolished" (Amos 3:15).

There's a hint here that in calling the Egyptians to see Israel's sins, God's people would be shocked into acknowledging the fact that they had been behaving worse than one of their heathen enemies. But what is really clear is that those who had gotten rich from oppressing others were going to be the ones paying the price. When our values come into conflict with God's, there is only one wise way to turn.

The prophecy shifts to the subject of worship, of the way in which the Israelites had become good at "doing" religion. It's obvious that God's chosen people had created a pleasantly cozy world for themselves, one in which worship was about ritual and form rather than heart and humility. Their religion was completely separated from God's laws, and Amos 2:7 points out their hypocrisy, as their worship was the soundtrack to the way "they trample[d] on the heads of the poor as on the dust of the ground and den[ied] justice to the oppressed."

What mattered more than quality religious services was their lifestyle. Sadly, all their singing and sacrificing didn't help them live better lives. This passage is still true for us today. We are so easily caught up in our own worlds, constructing our lives and investing energy in things we believe to be so vitally important but which fall so far short of God's plans. Israel was too self-absorbed to consider the consequences of lifestyle, and the truth is if they had been obedient, justice would have flowed, giving life to all around.

If we want to know whether our lifestyle choices are in line with God's agenda, the answer is a deafening NO if our actions cause others to be oppressed, impoverished, harmed, or exploited. In these days of the global supply chain and bargains made possible by sweatshop labor, this is a challenge we all face.

There is one final part of the Amos story that needs to be touched upon before moving on. The final round of prophecies started with something incredible: God told Amos about a plan to unleash a plague of locusts. But this wasn't just any plague—this one would wipe out all the land. Total destruction. But Amos prayed, pleading with God not to let it happen—and amazingly, God agreed. Then the pattern repeated, this time with a threat of a fire that would destroy all life. God again backed down when Amos prayed, and we can assume that He never wanted to destroy His creation. With this, a little hope crept in and Amos' prophecies carried on. Without destruction, how would it all end for God's people? Like Abraham questioning God, Amos assumed a sense of responsibility for his fellow men. More than just a mouthpiece, he became an agent of change, an upright believer, a true disciple of God.

....

God's math, part one: divine blessing + you ≠ big cash prizes

So what counts in God's scheme of things is not that we get rich by exploiting others, but that our faith increases human justice. It's also important that we recognize God as the ultimate Owner of all things and break out of the myopic mindset that allows us to focus solely on our own needs, wants, or obsessions. Sounds pretty simple to me.

But not according to some. For those who subscribe to the prosperity gospel, the Bible gives clear evidence of God's plan to make those He loves truly rich. Like all lies, there's a hint of truth in it, and precedent has paved the way with the likes of biblical heroes such as Abraham, Joseph, and David—great men of God who also found themselves on the receiving end of a swollen bank balance. But if we think their story ends there, we deceive ourselves. If we roll over and give in to the theory that God will reward our faith with financial bounty, we become just another set of narrow-minded, self-obsessed believers. We see relationship with God as the path along which we must travel toward the prize of material reward—not the reward itself.

Of course, it's appealing to sign up for the idea that God will make us rich, and again, I must state that I don't think having money is a bad thing. But it is certainly not the main thing. Though it begins neutral, it so easily can become something with either a positive or negative influence.

When it comes to slating the prosperity gospel, it's generally middle-class people like me who shout louder than those who know

10 MILLION:
Number of Americans with two or more homes

300,000+:
Number of homeless Americans[1]

true financial hardship. I don't know why God makes some people wealthier than others, and I would hate to criticize those whose faith has seen them through hardship. I guess I just struggle when believers conspire to create a cozy world from which God's concern for the poor gets easily squeezed out. Even though I belong to a part of the Church that flinches from telling believers that they'll get rich just as long as they believe enough, I know we have plenty of our own issues to deal with.

Whatever side of the material fence we sit on, it seems to me that the Church ought to spend far more time honing a broader outlook on such issues. We need to wake up to the fact that the consequences of our financial policies are spiritual issues, ones that are part of our faith. So when we see rising levels of personal debt and an increasing gulf between rich and poor, we as the people of God ought to be engaging in the debate and offering solutions that say more than "if you ask, then you will receive." We need to wake up to our responsibility to hold lightly to the things that sparkle and to

> **Proverbs 21:15**
> When justice is done, it brings joy to the righteous but terror to evildoers.

chase down the real heavenly prizes. If we ask, then we do receive— but do we necessarily receive what we ask for?

The reality is that throughout the Bible, money is never portrayed solely as a gift in isolation. It is a responsibility, a tool to help carry out even greater work for God. But it never gets top billing as a freebie that comes without responsibility. What's more, the lack of money is a great concern to Him. Those who have plenty of it can be tempted into believing that what the Bible calls poverty is not merely about financial restrictions or a lack of ready cash. We can delude ourselves by saying that people can be poor in all sorts of ways: having poor health, poor relationships, or poor prospects. True enough, but the Bible refuses to let us get away with absolving ourselves of responsibility for the impact that our lives have on others.

Poverty is a constant theme, and a specific one, too. Let's kick off with some study and a grateful thanks to Ron Sider's excellent book *Rich Christians in an Age of Hunger*. In Hebrew, the Old Testament uses a few words for the poor: *anaw, ani, dal, ebyon,* and *ras.* Between them, they define some fairly specific circumstances, like someone who is wrongfully impoverished or dispossessed; a beggar imploring charity; or a thin, weak, deprived peasant. By the time we get to the New Testament, the main word used for the poor is *ptochos*, meaning someone who is completely destitute and must take help from others. Ptochos is the Greek equivalent of ani or dal, which allows us to say that the main definition of the poor throughout Scripture relates to being of low economic status, usually due to some form of disaster or oppression.

So if not having money is a concern to God, doesn't logic dictate that those under His care should have it in abundance? Unfortunately, His plans are a tad more radical than this idea of rich Christians and poor heathens. Take a look back at the God-given mandate for a revolving cycle of ownership, as described in the Year of Jubilee (Lev. 25, Deut. 15). With the passing of every fifty years comes the canceling of debts, the return of all property to its original owners, and a chance for the soil to restock its resources as the land lies fallow. Ownership is God's, after all, and any ideas of personal empires run against the grain.

In addition to this radical plan to keep all members of society on a relatively equal footing, the rest of the Bible reinforces the importance of how we handle our money. With 2,350 verses on the subject, cash tops the charts, way above other such fundamental foundations of our beliefs as faith (500 verses) and prayer (about 500 verses).

Money is not necessarily linked to prosperity; it can be a barrier to faith, as it was for the rich young ruler who rejected Christ's offer of relationship in favor of maintaining his high level of account credit. It can be an offense to God, as Jesus made clear when He rebuked the money changers in the temple. When Simon the ex-sorcerer tried to buy himself a supersized blessing in Acts 8, he was told that he was bitter, wicked, captive to sin, and in serious need of repentance because his "heart [was] not right" (Acts 8:21). When the heart is wrong and the values out of line with God's own agenda, money clearly takes on negative properties.

When we look at biblical figures who were financially prosperous, we see men and women of God who were used because of their heart rather than their pocket. They were faithful servants whose wealth was transitory, incidental, or irrelevant to the bigger story. Money can only ever be a bit player in a greater feature, as it was with Esther. Her tremendous wealth was a signifier of influence—something that came with the job—but the real jewel was her boldness in trying to save her people. Joseph and Daniel were elevated to positions of power and influence, but this in itself did not serve as the real reward. Their power was the gate for opportunity, not simply luxury. Cash and currency brought the chance for convictions to shine through and for social change to roll out.

What we can be sure about is that when it is linked to injustice, money's value is negative, yet when used well, it can be extremely positive. In this way it is passive. It can be manipulated for good or bad and pass infection over to the holder. As Paul clearly states in 1 Timothy, it is the love of money that causes such harm. Money and financial rewards and material possessions are simply not worthy of our love; they are beneath such high esteem and devotion. We cannot allow ourselves to give our hearts, our passions, our energy, and our ideals to the pursuit of money. For beings who were created for friendship with God, our small worlds of cash and consumerism are a pale replacement of the glory of God's gravity.

God's math, part two: relationship with God > relationship with money

It's ironic: the chapter started off talking about the way in which we make our world too small, and we've ended up focusing on the single issue of wealth and material possessions. But perhaps this is where we need to start—by looking hard at the attitudes that have infused our subconscious. There can be no doubt that as an economic system, capitalism is intrinsically linked to our human weakness for materialism. Together, these two big hitters impact almost every aspect of our lives. Perhaps money really does have such a hold on us that it can distort our faith and distract from the ultimate prize, the bigger picture, and the real force of God's power.

In the last section of Matthew 18, starting with verse 21, Peter asks Jesus about forgiveness. In response, Jesus talks about money. First he tells Peter that he needs to forgive "seventy-seven times" (Matt. 18:22). That bit of coded language would have been understood by any Jew; since seven is the number linked with godly perfection, seventy-seven (or seventy times seven, as some translations have it) stands for infinity. In other words, there should be no standby button for the mercy we hand out to others.

But we're digressing. Jesus tells a story, a symbolic one about a king who wants to settle his accounts. He calls in a guy whose debt is of astronomical proportions (10,000 talents). He can't pay, so the king says he's going to sell him and his family and all their possessions in order to cover the debt. The man cries. He begs for mercy and promises to come up with the cash. The king feels kind, so he lets the man go, canceling the debt entirely. Later the freshly unburdened man finds a fellow servant who owes him money—but only a small amount (100 denarii). He starts to throttle this unlucky servant, demanding the money back, and the servant asks for a little more time. Sadly, the guy with the big debt has remarkably small reserves of both memory and compassion and, refusing his request, chucks the other guy into prison. Of course, the king finds out about all this and is, understandably, a trifle miffed. He has the first guy tortured, reinstates the debt he has just canceled, and sends a powerful lesson out to the rest of the community.

It's just a story, but the illustration packs a punch. The sums it deals with are huge. We know that King Herod was reported to earn 900 talents per year, so the debt of 10,000 talents is outrageously large. It was the equivalent of millions, even billions—a pile of silver weighing more than 300 tons or 350,000 kilos. The 100 denarii was worth one-millionth of the big debt, making it a relatively small amount that, unlike the 10,000 talents, could be paid back over time.

Jesus' message to Peter is clear: God has forgiven your sins, which was a colossal price to pay. Anything done against you is, by comparison, small change and should be forgiven fully.

So how does this apply to us and money? The second servant had a perfectly legal right to imprison his debtor—the law was on his side. But God wasn't. Why? Because relationship with God is more significant than relationship with money. Because God's bigger picture outranks our small world any day of the week. With our concept of ownership and limited funds for forgiveness and compassion, we can so easily become tight-fisted, narrow-minded, closed-hearted members of the faith. It simply is not supposed to be this way.

Finally, let's draw back to Job for a minute. His wealth stretched beyond the imagination of most, and yet the point of his story has so very little to do with his bank balance. His rapid descent into poverty and emotional chaos failed to throw him off course. His swift familiarization with pain and tragedy did not manage to dampen his devotion. His grief did not neutralize his praise. Surely these are the hallmarks of a man worth following—the ability to submit to God's gravity even when it feels as though every last ounce of goodness in life is getting stripped away. Satan was mistaken when he thought that poverty would rob Job of his devotion, but God knew otherwise. And when it was all over, Job ended up with twice as much wealth as he had before. Yet is that really to be taken as a sign of success—the old man on his deathbed, slipping away peacefully among the trappings of wealth and influence? Hardly. Job had experienced the truth. He had stood face to face with God and searched for the words in the silence that followed his Creator's questions. Surely God's affirmation was enough to last a lifetime.

LIVING THE RIGHT WAY UP

It is one of those days when I'm really not in the mood for one of God's challenges. Life is hard—a rough blend of pressures and stresses and worries and sorrow. It is gray, a question of making it through the hours to make it through the day. So when I turn up at Tearfund headquarters to interview a guy about his work with AIDS orphans in Temba, South Africa, I am determined to get in and out as quickly as possible.

Within five minutes I know that my wish will go unfulfilled. Gareth Kingdon— the man in question—is just wrapping up a story about how he has been involved in helping AIDS orphans in Temba, a township near Johannesburg.

"So we visited the local zoo and asked if we could have as much dung as they could spare."

Gareth, it would seem, is a little unusual. Actually, forget that—he's more than unusual. He's a twenty-year-old Christian from Cardiff, Wales, with a solid determination to put his beliefs into action. He does what he can, where he can, without making a big deal of it. And eight weeks before our meeting, Gareth was diagnosed with cystic fibrosis, a disease that may well mean he won't live beyond his thirties.

"When they told me that I had it, I went through a kind of trial, a period of feeling bad," Gareth says. "I realize now why there are so many psalms saying to God, 'Where are You?' That was how I felt, but after about an hour something changed, and I was full of joy and happiness."

For Gareth, that line in James 1 where we are told to rejoice in all our suffering made perfect sense. As he says, "I count it a privilege to have insight—even if it is brief—into how other people might feel about their suffering."

But I'm not there to dig up treats in order to turn him into some kind of poster boy for global compassion. Talking to him, I get the impression that while everything has changed for him since discovering

> "For those who believe in Jesus Christ, there is no death and no sorrow that is not mixed with hope—no despair—there is only constant being born again and going from darkness to light."
> —Vincent van Gogh

his illness, there are many ways in which life is still the same—the same old push to do something with his faith, the same old battle with frustration, and using those feelings to spur him on to action.

Growing up, Gareth developed a passion for South Africa, particularly the township of Temba, where his father often visited to preach and do what he could to help. Eventually, Gareth wanted to do things for himself, but "four years ago I was frustrated with having no money. I wanted to help but didn't know what to do."

One day an idea came to him. As an artist, he wondered if he might be able to raise a little cash by putting on an exhibition at his church. As soon as he had that thought, "I wondered whether there might be other artists in my church who would be willing to join in and show some of their art. And then it suddenly occurred to me that if there were people at my church who would be interested, then surely there must be people at other churches who would do the same. So it kind of grew."

The project went national, raising cash and awareness at the same time.

"Whether you're a DJ, a painter, a musician, or whatever, you can use your God-given creativity," Gareth says, becoming excited at the very mention of God's gifts.

Gareth's stories are wonderful and crazy and inspirational. The whole dung incident happened when they discovered that paper made out of elephant dung was going down well in the tourist shops around Johannesburg. If doing the same meant that people would be able to make a little money to support themselves, then Gareth wanted to get his hands on as much of the stuff as possible.

"AT CABELLO'S FUNERAL THERE WERE GRAVES AS FAR AS THE EYE COULD SEE."

But just as it is time to go, the mood changes a little. Time for another story, but this time it isn't funny. It is about a two-year-old boy named Cabello who died of AIDS. He spent his final week in the hospital, in a crib with two other children, one with tuberculosis and the other with nothing wrong at all—he was simply being "looked after" while his mother was in the psychiatric unit. All three were covered with urine and feces.

"That ward had sixteen beds in it," Gareth says, "and do you know how many people died there the previous month?"

I don't.

"Seventy." He pauses. "At Cabello's funeral there were graves as far as the eye could see, and on the graves were the people's favorite belongings. Like Cabello's, many of the graves had children's toys on top."

The image is almost too much to imagine. Time for one more story, a short one.

"In KwaZulu Natal, they're digging twenty-four hours a day just to have enough graves to cope with the AIDS victims."

The interview is over. It is time to go.

CHAPTER FIVE

Our World
Is Too Safe

We like safety. Not the wearing-a-crash-helmet-whenever-playing-Frisbee variety, but the deeper, more instinctive type. Somewhere inside us all is a primal fear of getting hurt, a subconscious allergic reaction to anything that threatens our security. Of course, it's all very understandable. Keeping away from things that threaten to hurt makes sense and is an obvious course of action to take. But there's a problem with it too, something that crops up whenever we transplant our attitudes toward the physical world onto our attitudes toward the spiritual. We end up flinching back from trial, fleeing from pain, seeing suffering as a sign of failure. For some in the Church it appears to be clear that tsunamis and hurricanes and epidemics are nothing less than vehicles of God's judgment. In the same way that prosperity-gospel fans believe that God's people will be blessed with material riches, supporters of the safety gospel suggest that God's people will live long and safe and free, just as long as the devil isn't snapping at their heels. Whichever way we try to dress it up, the end result is always an ill-fitting, badly coordinated mess.

Of course, there's something in all this. It is right and natural that we should resist anything that reminds us of death. After all, death was never meant to be part of the plan. Genesis makes it clear that God's early plan for mankind was just a little different from the current version we're riding. God's world was perpetual, eternal. Things existed in harmony, with balance and peace resting over all that had been made. Only after the fatal flaws of humankind came to the surface was death introduced. The serpent's mortality was presented when God suggested that it would crawl on its belly "all the days of [its] life" (Gen. 3:14). Reproduction came into being, the cycle of birth and death and pain set in motion as Eve became a mortal mother. Like the serpent, Adam received harsh words marking all the days of his life with destructive elements: painful toil, thorns, thistles, and sweat. He was given the ultimate physical destiny of having to return to earth. Suddenly Adam seemed a little less made in the image of God. Suddenly he was nothing more than shadows and dust.

THE FUNDAMENTAL PROBLEM WITH MY HEAD WAS THIS: I THOUGHT THAT GOD WAS ON MY SIDE. IT NEVER OCCURRED TO ME THAT THINGS MIGHT BE THE OTHER WAY AROUND, THAT THIS WHOLE CREATED ORDER MIGHT NOT SIMPLY REVOLVE AROUND ME.

The introduction of death changed things. The first couple became self-conscious, embarrassed, and ashamed, and it did not suit them well. They were less than they were meant to be, an inferior model downgraded after earlier production problems. They were meant for so much more, yet ended up so much less. Death was never supposed to be part of the plan. We shifted from the eternal to the temporal, from friends of God to those too muddied by sin to stand face to face with Him. We resisted the offer of unity and chose to pursue our own appetites. Of course we want to cover up and clothe ourselves with things that will protect us.

But there's a problem: we take things too far. In recoiling from death and suffering, we place ourselves on a track that can lead us to some fairly unreliable destinations. The logic can go in various directions, often traveling along the subconscious underground of our thought. I used to believe that if I prayed hard enough, life would be great. Okay, so I was young and impressionable and writing bad poetry in my spare time, but I really did believe it, deep down. I thought that God wanted me not only safe, but comfortable too. I though that the almighty Creator and Author of all things was on my side, backing me up as I picked my way through the perilous battles of service.

Things easily got out of hand. I remember when I used to routinely pray for the availability of perfect parking spaces or oh-so-ripe fruit at the supermarket. "Please, God," I would beg, "let me find just two perfectly ripe avocados today. And, by the way, You didn't really come up trumps on the parking spot, so if You could arrange for me to have at least a few green lights on the way back, I think we can call it even."

The fundamental problem—or at least one of the many fundamental problems—with my head at the time was this: I thought that God was on my side. It never occurred to me that things might be the other way around, that this whole created order might not simply revolve around me. Instead—and this is where I had a bit of a crash landing with reality—we're part of God's supporting cast, here to join in and sign up to fight His battles, rather than picking our own and expecting Him to clean up. These days I don't know if God cares about parking spaces or ingredients for a good guacamole, but if He does, I'm sure He'll let me know.

The roots of it all

So, this is a rally cry for misery? A two-minute warning for desperation and suffering? Of course not. It is right that we pursue life and resist the things that will harm us, but there's a danger more potent than a bumpy career path or a house purchase that falls through at the last minute. There are consequences that are far longer-lasting and significant when we begin to equate suffering with failure, when we consider that God's part of the deal will be to serve us up a blessed, happy, and highly favored life. The narrow-minded approach didn't work for Adam and Eve, and it failed to get a look in with Jesus. But even though few of us would openly admit to the belief that Christianity is a passport to a hassle-free life, are we really so sure that we've got things the right way up? Are we sure that we're not inclined toward reaching for our Mary Poppins Jesus whenever we need a spoonful of sugar to help life's harsh medicine go down?

Our gravity pulls us toward the things that lend us a sense of security. Of course it does. Why wouldn't it? But God's variety is another matter altogether. As Michael Lloyd suggests in *Café Theology*, even before all that business with Adam, Eve, the snake, and the apple, things had started to go wrong. The serpent made his way into the garden, breaking into paradise. Adam had been given the command to subdue and rule over what God had made. Eden itself was in the east, an oasis that is, by implication, different and better than the rest of the earth—the very place deemed "good" just a few verses earlier. Together, these three facts seem to suggest that even before man messed up, God's plan for the earth was not being carried out. Lloyd suggests that the fall started before all of this, that things had started to go wrong when the angels began to rebel. With a number of them getting expelled from heaven, something dramatic happened. Cracks appeared in the plaster, and chaos and disharmony entered the frame.[1]

Did God mess up? If I were in charge of the project, I'd be inclined to trash the model and go back to the beginning. Yet God—as I am becoming ever more glad with the passing of years—is not like me. God chose to keep what He had created, to invest yet more of Himself in the beings that were already offering such a pale imitation of the glory He had intended for them. We turned our backs, yet God offered His pillar of fire to guide us. We closed our hearts, so God sent His Son. We tortured and killed Him, yet God sent His Spirit. I obsess about parking spots and avocados, yet God still wants me to know Him.

There are a billion reasons for God to give up on us, yet He simply refuses to do so.

ARE WE SURE THAT WE'RE NOT INCLINED TOWARD REACHING FOR OUR MARY POPPINS JESUS WHENEVER WE NEED A SPOONFUL OF SUGAR TO HELP LIFE'S HARSH MEDICINE GO DOWN?

What does this mean for us? Surely it gives all the more glory to God, elevating Him even higher above us with our narrow minds and fuzzy outlooks. Believing that God can still be God without expecting Him to conform to our obsessions with control is a big leap to make, and those who struggle to do so find themselves staring at the chasm in confused isolation. They suggest that the presence of suffering—the tsunamis, the genocides, the evil that is plainly wrong in our world—indicates that God is cruel, that His passive acceptance of wrongdoing must mean He is callous, absent, or weak. But seeing God as a divine protector is not right. Such a being is not a god, but a fairy-tale guardian, a fairy godmother who won't even let the pumpkin return at the stroke of midnight. God's gravity is strong— but with a type of strength that goes beyond our narrowly defined expectations. With His power comes our freedom, allowing us the greatest responsibility of all—choice. In other words, we can choose to be pulled into His orbit, or we can choose to pursue our own.

But why would He do this? Because God is all about the relationship. From the early accounts in Genesis we see God as a uniquely personal force behind creation. From verse 1 it is clear that in the beginning God created the world. Not gas or energy, randomness or accident ... but God. Whether or not you take this literally is beside the point. What counts is that God chose to reveal Himself as the ultimate Author, the eternal Creator, the essential Father that witnessed the birth of the world. He is the Alpha and the Omega, the beginning and the end, the reason why all this makes sense. Why would God create? Because giving life and sharing it is the inevitable consequence of His goodness. Because He wanted to create and to share. Because if we were made for relationship, then God exists for it, too.

Evil, suffering, and death occur not because this was how God wanted things to be, but because this is exactly how He didn't want it. God did not want suffering or chaos or the mortality that plagues us, but human actions made these an inevitable consequence. Because mankind was created with free will and the ability to make their own decisions, Adam and Eve were able to disobey God's command to steer clear of the fruit of the tree of the knowledge of good and evil, much as the angels were able to rebel. It is to our actions, our selfishness, our flawed behavior that we must look to if we want an answer as to why there is suffering in the world. The finger of blame does not belong in God's direction, but our own.

> "True peace is not merely the absence of tension: it is the presence of justice."
> —Martin Luther King Jr.

By choosing to pull free of God's gravity, we have allowed our selfishness to affect everything. It altered the quality of relationship between Adam and Eve and God, causing the humans to hide in shame (Gen. 3:8). It messed things up between Adam and Eve, as they struggled with blame and power (Gen. 3:12, 16). After the fall it was clear that family relationships were a little strained; Genesis 4:1–8 tells of the horrific incident that left Abel bloodied and dead in a field at the hands of his brother, Cain. The environment seemed to struggle with mankind too, refusing to offer its fruits easily (Gen. 3:17–19). Finally Adam and Eve's bodies started to rebel, offering pain and troubles up to the final moment of death. None of this makes for much of a pretty picture. Of course we are going to want things to be different. God does, too.

God refuses to leave it there, and we cannot look at the fall of man without turning our attention to the rise of God's Son. While our wayward actions explain why there is suffering, Jesus' life and death help place it in context and show precisely how God refuses to leave it at that. Hands nailed open, Jesus' pose indicates the symbolic as well as the literal: He was embracing suffering, not turning away from it.

Choosing to turn away from suffering and hardship feels comforting; embracing it goes against our instincts. But unless we break through the pain barrier and reframe our approach to things, we will find it impossible to truly have a relationship with God. Jesus on the cross with His arms outstretched, willing to accept the suffering in front of Him, signals the way forward. This is Christ saying to His followers, "Come," inviting us to join Him.[2] And if we can't acknowledge His suffering, if we can't see our part in putting Him on the cross, then we simply cannot take up the offer of relationship. If we are to embrace Him, we must embrace the cross as well, with all its suffering and sacrifice.

So should we expect to have to go through the same pain? Will we all end up tortured and destroyed by cruel hands? We are certainly told to take up our own crosses. The Gospels repeatedly show Jesus telling His followers that unless they follow His example, their kind words and keen hearts count for nothing (Matt. 10:38, 16:24; Mark

8:34; Luke 9:23, 14:27). If we follow Christ, we can expect some of the same. Yet there is more to the cross than pain, even more than death. Without the resurrection, Christ's story would be just another folktale, with the cross the tool that won out over a fragile, broken body. With the empty tomb and the resurrection, the cross becomes a uniquely different symbol. It shows us that Christ is stronger than suffering, that He is bigger than death. It speaks of bravery and acceptance and sacrifice. Yes, there is tremendous pain involved, but that is a bit part that fails to take the final limelight. The cross now represents a place where broken hearts are restored, relationships cemented, and responsibilities spelled out. John was told to care for Mary; Jesus' command turns the tables on the fall. The message is clear: our world should not begin and end with meeting our own selfish needs. What counts is the bigger picture—even if it involves having things go against our plans.

Is negative emotion off the menu?

Remember Jesus in torment outside the tomb of Lazarus? We read that upon seeing the grief of Lazarus' friends and family, Jesus "was deeply moved in spirit and troubled" (John 11:33). This death clearly upset Him. But it is also clear that He did not fear God's reaction; He was not trying to hide His tears for fear that God might pull Him up for being weak-willed or off-message. With tears and sobs, Jesus prayed: "Father, I thank you that you have heard me. I knew that you always hear me, but I said this for the benefit of the people standing here, that they may believe that you sent me" (John 11:41–42).

There are times when suffering is wrong. There are times when it is to be railed against, resisted, and rejected. Yet do we roll all this out with an attitude of anger and resentment toward God? Not if we're following Jesus' model here. His grief walked hand in hand with gratitude. Perhaps that is the way we, too, should relate to the presence of pain and suffering—to recognize it for what it is, with praise, worship, and trust close behind.

....

What makes God angry?

It would be wrong to paint suffering as a solely neutral force. At times it can exist as a form of divine judgment. Want proof? From Noah's drowned peers to Sodom and Gomorrah's corpses, from Pharaoh's multitude of plagues to the threats handed out via Amos, the God of the Old Testament made it clear that His displeasure could be expected in acts that seem almost incomprehensibly cruel. Can we reconcile the two sides of God—the Old Testament authoritarian and the New Testament radical peacenik?

Painting God as some kind of bipolar reject from the anger management school simply won't do. Look back across the Old Testament at the way He interacted with His chosen people, and it is possible to see the links across the two halves of Scripture. God's protection of His people and punishment of their oppressors go hand in hand. He rescued the Israelites from the Egyptians, yet this was not a sign that they could live happily ever after in a vacuum where their actions attracted no consequence. God's passion for justice brought them freedom, but when they in turn became oppressors, they were threatened with destruction and judgment in even greater measure. In deciding to align themselves to their own gravity, to pursue idolatry and oppression, the chosen people of God kicked off a game of tag. The Israelites were constantly finding themselves getting pulled back to their knees by the prophets, only to rise back up and wander off again.

By the time Amos was told to wake them up to their wrongdoings, their lifestyle was a mess. As we have already seen, their worship may have been slick, but injustice and oppression were rife. As Ronald

Sider points out, archaeological discoveries about housing extremes indicate that the gap between rich and poor was significant in the eighth century BC. Within just two centuries, the gap between rich and poor had increased to such an extent that God's passion for justice yet again overruled human desire for safety, protection, and prosperity. We know that Amos brokered a deal, acting as the agent that alerted many to the vital importance of human justice, but God still allowed a degree of suffering as an inevitable consequence of the Israelites' choices. The savage Assyrians conquered the Northern Kingdom. God's judgment on their lifestyle was clear: He would not stand for it.[3]

Entering God's orbit

I once heard a talk where the vicar suggested that when life gets tough, we need only to determine whether the cause of our difficulties is God or the devil. Are we being tested or attacked? At that time my life was hard; my wife took up a daily, even hourly, struggle against the ravages of postpartum depression. Who or what was behind this? We never really did make up our minds. But one thing came out of the experience: without trust in God, we have nothing that will weather the storms that life brings us. Seeing the world as an imperfect reflection of God's created order may help us refocus our perspective, draw the camera back, and see the truth that pain and difficulty are not necessarily signs of failure, but rather consequences of our own fallen actions.

When troubles arise, perhaps we should adopt the approach Christ took in front of both His own and Lazarus' tombs. Both were surrounded by grief, yet the power of the Almighty was more than enough to roll away the stone. Both were thought to be final endings, yet they were merely essential parts of the plot, pit stops on the way to a greater destiny. Both revealed Jesus communicating with God, caring for others, and righting the wrongs of a discordant world. Perhaps that is how we should approach the trials of life: instead of remaining motionless in front of or within our tombs, wallowing in pain or refusing to move on, we should step out or cry out in thanks and grief. The process is hard and costly—yet without it, we reduce the power of the cross, the power that resurrects and redirects, to a meaningless token.

Our world is too safe. God's gravity pulls us toward a bigger, bolder, brighter orbit. What counts out there is our service rather than our protection, our sacrifice rather than our safety, our decision not to turn away from but to face and embrace the outstretched arms nailed to the cross.

GLIMPSES

IN SEARCH OF SAFETY

Colombia is not a safe place to live. With rival factions fighting for control of land, drugs, and people, murder is the fabric of daily life: the death toll reaches a colossal twenty-eight thousand every year. Yet even by Colombia's standards, the city of Medellín is particularly dangerous—so much so that local residents dub it the city of eternal gunfire.

Meet Johan, a twenty-one-year-old who was smoking crack and carrying a gun by the time he was eleven. But this was not some kind of trite imitation of gangsta-rap attitude; this was real life. His family tree is a classic illustration of lives cut short by violent deaths. His brothers spent their teens as part of rival groups, caught up in a life of gun running, robbery, and kidnapping. One was tortured, his body sent back to his gang in a coffin. He had been burned with an iron.

In a country where primary-school-aged kids can be hired as assassins, the typical reaction would be to seek revenge. Yet Johan started along another path, one that laid down the greater challenge of forgiving others.

A friend had introduced him to Club Deportivo, a local soccer club run by Christians.

"I started training with the team, and I loved it. They started talking to me about God. I thought this was completely ridiculous, and I hated it that they talked to me about God. They made us pray and study the Bible. I just did it to go with the flow, not because it came from my heart."

Yet one day, things changed. Having accepted the challenge to go to church, he found himself face to face with a life-transforming message.

"They talked about the fact that Jesus wasn't religion; He was a completely different way of life. He could change my life if I accepted Him into my heart."

And he did. That was six years ago, and now Johan works as a coach at the project, giving teenagers a sense of purpose, self-discipline, and hope. Forgiving others as Jesus taught us is not easy, but Johan knows that it's the only way forward for the youth of Medellín. He's clear about the challenge that forgiveness poses for teenagers like Andrés, who was caught in the crossfire of a local gun battle and has been left almost paralyzed. Or Fabian, whose faith helped him through the trauma of getting shot in the hand and chest while out with his girlfriend. Or María, who, at seventeen, is still mourning the loss of

COLOMBIA FACTS:
Ten families are forced to flee their homes every hour.

More than two million people have left their communities during the forty-year civil war.

More than seventeen thousand people have been kidnapped over the last five years.[4]

her father. He was a key member of a violent gang and was murdered after he defected. Through the likes of Johan and others at Club Deportivo, she is being shown an alternative way to react to the devastation around her.

"We would have joined an armed group to get vengeance," she says. "If you lose the most important person in your life, you don't care what you do to the person who did it."

Through prayer, commitment, forgiveness, and plenty of soccer, these lives are being changed. The Bible lays out a blueprint for forgiveness; Club Deportivo is starting to build a new Colombia based on God's plans.

CHAPTER SIX

Our World
Is Too Vain

If our world can be made too small by our pursuit of temporary treats and material highs, or too safe by our avoidance of trial and difficulty, then there is one more key trap into which we can fall, completing the trio of errors that constructs a me-first faith and takes us away from God's gravity. The third problem is vanity. We long for a mighty destiny without ever considering the small steps that must be taken to reach it.

Take a look at the lives of four remarkable Christians—William Seymour, Nelson Mandela, C.T. Studd, and Perpetua—and you may be impressed by the headline features of their biographies rather than the quality of their daily, mundane selfless sacrifice. Because they are heroes of the faith, we may wish to concentrate on their final destination, instead of the process that got them there. Yet while a big destiny may be infinitely sexier than a quiet life of unimpressive service, it simply does not tie up with God's idea of things. With each of these four heroes, their small steps offer a clear path to follow.

William Seymour is rightly called the father of the modern Pentecostal movement. Today's 400 million Pentecostal and Charismatic believers can trace their spiritual roots directly back to his work in the first decade of the twentieth century. What matters is his life, not the headlines. The son of ex-slaves, blind in one eye, betrayed, abused, and rejected, Seymour refused to compromise on the practical, sacrificial, costly task he knew God had placed in front of him. No matter how many times the white Christian leaders, motivated by jealousy and racial hatred, turned on Seymour, he kept the faith. He brought races together to meet in the power of the Holy Spirit in a way that has transformed Christianity ever since. Yet at his death his once-famous church contained just one or two dozen believers, his influence scattered and his reputation forgotten. William Seymour's final words said it all, summing up his integrity and passion in spite of a lifetime of struggle and service. As the breath escaped his body he said this: "I love my Jesus so."[1]

> "Washing one's hands of the conflict between the powerful and the powerless means to side with the powerful, not to be neutral."
>
> —Paulo Freire

Another black leader has a significantly higher profile today, yet Nelson Mandela's role as South Africa's reconciler, shepherd, and leader did not come without a price. In 1964 Mandela stood trial, a possible death sentence hanging over him. His closing words to the court astounded the nation:

"During my lifetime I have dedicated myself to this struggle of the African people. I have fought against white domination, and I have fought against black domination. I have cherished the ideal of a democratic and free society in which all persons live together in harmony and with equal opportunities. It is an ideal which I hope to live for and to achieve. But if needs be, it is an ideal for which I am prepared to die."[2]

Twenty-seven years in prison did not leave him bitter, angry, or determined for retribution. Instead, it honed and refined, producing a man who struggled for unity and justice, despite the threat of opposition.

Then there is C. T. Studd. Educated at the cream of Britain's educational establishments, Eton College and then Cambridge, he went on to captain the English cricket team and appeared on course for a life of wealth and privilege, thanks to his father's phenomenal financial resources. At eighteen Studd became a Christian, but it was not until he turned twenty-five that he finally made the decision to take his faith seriously. Choosing a radical life of sacrifice and generosity, Studd gave away his entire inheritance and took the Gospel to China, India, and Sudan. Without his work the global reach of today's Church would be radically different, yet it was his generosity and determination that created his legacy. He died old and poor but gloriously rich in obedience and love of God. Speaking out against those who claimed that his final mission trip to Africa was sheer foolishness, he claimed, "Gentlemen, God has called me to go, and I will go. I will blaze the trail, though my grave may only become a stepping stone that younger men may follow."[3]

Perpetua, one of the earliest female Christian martyrs, was arrested for her faith in AD 203. Along with a handful of others, the twenty-two-year-old faced the death sentence. Visiting her in prison, her father urged her to reject her beliefs and save herself. He begged her to retract the words that would send her to her death, yet her reply was clear: "Can you call this water jug by any other name? No. I can't call myself anything other than what I am—a Christian."[4]

She followed her divine compass and was pulled toward the actions she knew to be right, showing dignity, courage, strength, and faith. She died as a wild animal attacked her to the cheers of the delighted crowd.

Seymour, Mandela, Studd, and Perpetua make up quite a crowd. They
are remarkable people who achieved remarkable things, yet the key
is so clear with each. Seymour chose to be open-handed, refusing
to hold on to the power that so quickly slipped through his fingers.
Mandela chose forgiveness, as almost three decades of his life ebbed
away at the whim of a cruel and oppressive regime. Studd chose to
be generous, to give away material possessions in spite of the value
society placed on his privileged position. Perpetua simply spoke the
truth, refusing to deny Christ, no matter what the cost. It is the small
steps that count, not the podium.

Striding against the tide

God plays by different rules than those who are in force around
us today. Instead of being impressed by the outcome of our effort,
He's more interested in the heart behind it. Rather than status and
significance, fame and fortune, it is obedience and sacrifice, humility
and devotion that are the truly impressive jewels. Nowhere is this
expressed more concisely than in the words Jesus spoke on the
mountainside:

> Blessed are the poor in spirit, for theirs is the kingdom
> of heaven. Blessed are those who mourn, for they will
> be comforted. Blessed are the meek, for they will inherit
> the earth. Blessed are those who hunger and thirst for
> righteousness, for they will be filled. Blessed are the
> merciful, for they will be shown mercy. Blessed are the pure
> in heart, for they will see God. Blessed are the peacemakers,
> for they will be called children of God. Blessed are those
> who are persecuted because of righteousness, for theirs is
> the kingdom of heaven. Blessed are you when people insult
> you, persecute you and falsely say all kinds of evil against
> you because of me. Rejoice and be glad, because great is

your reward in heaven, for in the same way they persecuted
the prophets who were before you. (Matt. 5:3–12)

What do we see here? A set of principles designed to shake the very
foundations of society. These were not fluffy remarks headed straight
for the nearest greeting card. Jesus was not talking about people in
general; He was speaking to the disciples about what to expect in life.
When they did end up poor, mourning, and hungry, they were not
to take it as a sign of punishment; they were to take it as blessing. It
worked the other way, too: possessions and comfy living would not
be signs of blessing. And this, said Jesus, is the way life will be. It's part
of the Jesus revolution. Has the revolution revolutionized us yet?

All this goes beautifully against the bold destinations that we admire,
the things we point to as evidence that someone has "made it." Jesus
spells out what
characterizes
the lives of the
followers of God,
pointing out the
signs that will
indicate that He
is blessing us. First
is the realization
that we're in

Percentage of Americans who say they have achieved the American Dream:

Those earning less than $15,000: 5%
Those earning more than $50,000: 6%[5]

dire need of God, that spiritually we have nothing (verse 3). There's
a willingness to engage in the pain of the world around us and the
sorrow at the state things are in (verse 4). There's a degree of humility,
a desire to put others before ourselves (verse 5), along with a striving
for justice and right behavior (verse 6). Jesus goes on to mention
forgiveness, kindness, and compassion (verse 7), as well as purity of
intentions and motives—a love for what is right and a determination
to keep out of evil (verse 8). We are to work as reconcilers, bringing
not conflict but unity (verse 9). Finally, we must be willing not to be

popular, not to be well thought of, but to face opposition because of Jesus (verse 10). This is what will happen if we follow Jesus. And when it does, we are not meant to take it as a sign that everything's going wrong. It actually means we're blessed.

These are the small steps that we are to take, the practical things we can do within the next twenty-four hours to move our lives closer to God's standard. While we might rather sit around and wonder when something remarkable is going to happen to us, these simple, obvious, unimpressive, and often unrecognizable actions and attitudes are the real path to true success.

Hezekiah: the good and the not-so-good

The Old Testament king Hezekiah understood this. And then he forgot it, which was a bit of a shame. At the age of thirty-seven or thirty-eight Hezekiah was told that his life was about to end. His achievements had been impressive: he had restored a passion for worship across the two divided kingdoms, reignited the Israelites' dedication to serving God instead of other idols, and depended on the Almighty for protection from the cruel Assyrians. It looked as though his life was about to be remembered for his dedicated service and obedience. But finding out that death was around the corner did not sit well with his soul:

"In those days Hezekiah became ill and was at the point of death. The prophet Isaiah son of Amoz went to him and said, 'This is what the Lord says: Put your house in order, because you are going to die; you will not recover.' Hezekiah turned his face to the wall and prayed to the Lord, 'Remember, Lord, how I have walked before you faithfully and with wholehearted devotion and have done what is good in your eyes.' And Hezekiah wept bitterly" (2 Kings 20:1–3).

Perhaps Hezekiah's tears were understandable, but they also revealed the heart of the man. Instead of regaling the Lord with a list of all his achievements, persuading God to extend his life by reciting his résumé, Hezekiah's prayer showed that he understood what God valued—a committed and faithful heart, rather than impressive tasks. In return, God performed a miracle using a medicinal remedy, and Hezekiah got another fifteen years added on to his life.

So far, so good. Yet there was room for a mistake, an act that revealed the classic pitfall into which we can so easily slip. Hezekiah messed up by entering into an unwise alliance with the Babylonians. It started when they paid him a visit, flattering him with letters and gifts. In return, Hezekiah took them on a tour of his storehouses of wealth, displaying the physical fruits of a lifetime on the throne. Isaiah was suspicious and probed the king:

> The prophet asked, "What did they see in your palace?"
> "They saw everything in my palace," Hezekiah said. "There is nothing among my treasures that I did not show them."
> Then Isaiah said to Hezekiah, "Hear the word of the Lord: The time will surely come when everything in your palace, and all that your predecessors have stored up until this day, will be carried off to Babylon. Nothing will be left, says the Lord. And some of your descendants, your own flesh and blood who will be born to you, will be taken away, and they will become eunuchs in the palace of the king of Babylon."
> (2 Kings 20:15–18)

It was as if Hezekiah had forgotten the values he had held on to while weeping on his temporary deathbed. Instead of maintaining an attitude of humble obedience to the Lord, he gave in to vanity, displaying the treasures that reflected his own glory rather than humbly serving God, preening himself in front of what he proudly called "my treasures."

Isaiah was right about the outcome. About 115 years after Hezekiah's death, God's people found themselves under the oppression of Nebuchadnezzar. According to Isaiah, the blame lay fairly and squarely at the feet of the king's moment of vanity.

More than our achievements, it is our heart that matters. More than our visible influence on the outcome, it is our hidden steps of service and humility that count. More than pandering to our own sense of vanity, it is by following God—putting Him first and our own gratification second on a daily basis—that we ever stand the chance of doing anything remotely worthy of note. God wants a lifestyle dedicated to Him. It might go against the grain and appear all wrong, but the glory of God has always been bound up in decidedly countercultural values.

The wrong story

We can see this even in something as sanitized as Christmas. Despite all our attempts to crowd out the God stuff with Santas and overindulgence and mass consumption, the story remains so very good because everything seems to go so wrong.

For the young couple, the scandal of pregnancy before marriage put them in one of society's "wrong" categories. The fifty-four-mile trek from Nazareth to Bethlehem was the wrong thing entirely for a pregnant woman at full term. The cattle shed was the wrong birth environment, and the socially unimpressive shepherds were altogether, well, wrong. Add the foreign astrologers, the hasty exodus to Egypt, and the separation from the support that a small town like Nazareth would have offered to a young family, and it's clear that God's choice of entrance for His flesh and blood plays by a decidedly alternative set of rules.

The Christmas story has plenty to teach us, even today. One thing is evident: by siding so clearly with such an undesirable set of circumstances, God places value on that which we so often despise. When we are tempted to separate ourselves from what we consider to bear the hallmark of failure, God embraces it as His own. While we might avoid, misunderstand, or fear those on the margins of society, the Gospel message exhorts us to stand alongside them.

WHEN WE ARE TEMPTED TO SEPARATE OURSELVES FROM WHAT WE CONSIDER TO BEAR THE HALLMARK OF FAILURE, GOD EMBRACES IT AS HIS OWN.

Fast-forward to the end of Christ's life, and the message is even clearer. We are told to love the unloved, to reach beyond that which is comfortable, and to be eyes to the blind, feet to the lame, a father to the needy—the sort of people intent on taking up the case of a stranger.

Throughout His life, Jesus' decision to align Himself with social misfits and outcasts challenged the wisdom of the day. Whether they were of the wrong sex, age, race, state of health, or career, Jesus' practical compassion—the offers of healing, defense, food, friendship—underlined the fact that His was a radical new message that was not meant for the few, but for the many.

As for what all this has to do with us, the answer is clear: our mandate is to walk side by side with those marginalized by society. Just as in the Middle East two millennia ago, today there is no shortage of "wrong" people to do the right thing for.

With its refusal to accept what society tells us is the right value to place on people and things, the Church has the mandate to transform the lives whom society has failed. Take a closer look at them—the asylum-seekers, the migrants, the homeless, the travelers, the poor, the lonely, the widowed, the orphaned, the hungry, and the naked—and it becomes clear: these are the people with whom our God chose to surround Himself. These are the people whom our God chose to live among. Not the people whose destiny was bound up in impressive headlines and personal achievement, but the broken and the despised, the wrong sort altogether.

Becoming part of the plan

Realizing that our inadequacy is greater than our ability is a vital stage for any Christian to reach. For Moses and Esther it was both profoundly uncomfortable and personally dangerous. Yet ironically, it was only when they acknowledged their dependence on God that their obedient actions placed them at the heart of profound social change.

The Israelites under Pharaoh's reign found themselves at the wrong end of a power system designed to protect the interests of those at the top. Fortunately for us, God's plans were bigger than the Egyptian restrictions, as Moses found out in person:

> The Lord said, "I have indeed seen the misery of my people in Egypt. I have heard them crying out because of their slave drivers, and I am concerned about their suffering. So I have come down to rescue them from the hand of the Egyptians and to bring them up out of that land into a good and spacious land, a land flowing with milk and honey ... And now the cry of the Israelites has reached me, and I have seen the way the Egyptians are oppressing them. So now, go. I am sending you to Pharaoh to bring my people the Israelites out of Egypt." (Exod. 3:7–10)

It all started off pretty well, with God apparently building up to some blockbuster action sequence where He took the oppressive Egyptians apart, piece by piece. As God declared that He had "seen the misery, heard the crying, and come down to rescue them," surely Moses would have been settling into his armchair and rubbing his hands in eager anticipation at the remarkable spectacle he was about to witness. Then came the twist, the four words that turned the tables completely: "I am sending you." This killer line, this counterpoint that shifted the tone as God placed Moses at the heart of His plan A, was completely unexpected, yet hugely appropriate. Of course Moses was unable to achieve the task; of course it was a ridiculous idea; of course Moses would be utterly dependent on God.

When God said, "I am sending you," it was *you* singular, not plural, that was used. *You* alone, impetuous, unwise, and wholly unqualified to do the job. *You*, overwhelmed and dwarfed by the task. I wonder if we can still hear the call today.

We know what followed. We know that God's power to save was more than enough without the input of Moses, but that through God's grace Moses was invited into partnership with Him, to be the waiter who delivered the order. We know that God sees current miseries, tears, and suffering. And when we know that it is God whom we must rely on. Perhaps we, too, can become the *you* at the heart of His plan.

Even more so than Moses, Esther was the wrong person for her mission—wrong race, wrong gender, wrong social status—yet she was perfect for the role of biblical heroine. Having been abducted from her home to satisfy the lust/alcoholism/commitment issues of King Xerxes of Persia, Esther was part of the restock of the royal harem. Though she had been advised to keep quiet about her Jewish status, it became a burning issue once her cousin Mordecai discovered a plot to slaughter the Jews in Persia. A desperate situation called for desperate measures, and Queen Esther took the potentially fatal step of entering her master's presence uninvited to plead for the lives of her people. It turned out, as her cousin had said, that she found herself with powerful access "for such a time as this."

The story appears to be making a resurgence in popularity today. It illustrates the potential influence that Christians can have and encourages us to speak out against injustice, to recognize that we too have been born for such a time as this. It's a wonderful soundbite and a tantalizing prospect. But we run the risk of pandering to our sense of vanity if we congratulate ourselves too much for being so marvelously well-connected and capable of effecting change.

> **Proverbs 29:7**
> The righteous care about justice for the poor, but the wicked have no such concern.

Mordecai knew this, too. As he presented Esther with her options and suggested that she use her influence over the unstable king, he got to the heart of the matter: "Do not think that because you are in the king's house you alone of all the Jews will escape. For if you remain silent at this time, relief and deliverance for the Jews will arise from another place, but you and your father's family will perish. And who knows but that you have come to royal position for such a time as this?" (Esther 4:13–14)

If Esther did not act, someone else would. She may have been queen, but she was not unique. She may have endured the outrageous hardship of abduction and sexual abuse, but she was not the only one who could help. Someone else would come along and act in her place. She was not indispensable.

If not us ... someone else will stand

This is the paradox of God's gravity. We have thought about the
importance of stepping up to the plate and assuming responsibility.
We have wondered about the differences between human and divine
justice. We have explored the ways in which, by putting God first, we
find ourselves in the right place—even if it appears wholly wrong to
our society's values. On the one hand, we know that what matters
in life is our service and obedience to God. There is no room for
vanity, arrogance, or pride. Yet on the other hand, the eternal truth
is this: God's power can transform not only our lives but those of
millions around us. Just one person who is dedicated to serving
and following God can effect change, the likes of which our self-
sufficient motivations could never hope to achieve. Moses, Esther,
even Seymour and the others may be heroes of the faith, yet their
remarkable outcomes were not marked by remarkable ability or skill.
What counted was simply their ability to follow and serve.

Of all the examples, the cross is the only true leader, and it too is
bound up in paradox. As a symbol of torture, it became the icon
of freedom. An agent of death became the gateway to life. The
punishment of man became the payment of God. The body splayed
out in vulnerability became the arms that are open to all who want
to approach God. The death of life became the birth of hope. This is
true godly success, caked in blood, bereft of dignity, shining in glory.

God's gravity will pull us toward something remarkable. It will pull
us toward relationship with Him, toward the only true source of
satisfaction and success that will ever count in life. Yet it will take us
away from that which the world values. It will make us weaker than
our peers, yet stronger than mountains. It will make us poorer than
we ought to be, yet richer than tycoons and kings combined. It will
make us less impressive, yet it will take us step by step to the only

destiny that matters. We can pull away from it at any time, yet God's gravity is a force to which nothing can compare.

TURNING THE TABLES

The Bible is not the first place you'd expect to find clear-cut advice on moneymaking schemes. But it's all there, a simple lesson in the art of turning a profit. And there's something else, too—it's not tucked away in one of the more dusty corners of the Good Book; it's right there, front and center, forming Jesus' grand finale before He ascended heavenward.

The parable of the talents (Matthew 25) tells the story of a boss who leaves a stack of cash in the care of his workers while he is away. And it is a lot of cash—one talent was equivalent to sixteen years of labor—that the crew of three is supposed to invest and increase over a period of time. The first two do well, multiplying their master's booty. Yet the third servant, rather than wisely using the single talent he has been given, buries it. Why? Because he is scared. Or at least that's what he says in the story. Perhaps he is lazy too, but either way, he gets a hefty verbal slap from the boss.

This story has an important lesson we can draw from: we must make the most of our opportunities and resources. It's no surprise that the word talent has taken on the particular meaning it has in today's language. We all have God-given talents we need to put to use.

But what if you can't use these skills and abilities? What if poverty has such a tight grip on you that you can't get out of it on your own?

This is what life is like for millions of people around the world. Caught in the cycle of poverty, all their energy has to be directed toward survival rather than into investing for a future.

Take Mithu, for instance. Without any education or training, he has to work for others for an income. Laborers like Mithu don't earn much in countries like Bangladesh, and the work itself is only available certain times of the year. He has to catch fish to help feed his family, but sometimes they still go hungry.

Bangladesh is home to one of the poorest populations on earth. It's also home to one of the most chaotic weather cycles, with floods and cyclones forming a sadly familiar, devastating script.

But there are ways out. Projects like the ones run by Heed are working to make a dramatic difference to the way the country looks.

The key is the sneaky little word sustainability. It doesn't mean the art of eating a decent breakfast, but rather boils down to the idea that people need something that will last for more than a day. There's an old saying that if you give a person a fish, you feed him for a day; but if you teach him how to use a rod and line, he'll feed himself for life. That's sustainability, and without it, the road out of poverty is truly blocked.

BANGLADESH FACTS:
44 percent of the population live below the poverty line.

The life expectancy is fifty-six years.

Every year, 300,000 people move to the capital city of Dhaka.

By 2015, Dhaka may be the fourth largest city in the world, with a population of twenty million.[6]

Chickens. That's the answer. Or at least it has been for many people working alongside Heed. You see, with just a loan, many people are able to work their way out of poverty, setting up a simple yet totally effective business. With the cash to buy a little land, people are able to buy a few chickens. Selling eggs raises the money to buy and plant seeds, which then leaves the farmer with a crop to sell. And by breeding chickens, the birds themselves become yet another potential source of income. All in all, for a little cash, they can set up a pretty tasty business.

Of course, some of you might notice a problem: how do they get the loan in the first place? With no land and no savings, a citizen hoping to leave a life of poverty behind does not make for a particularly attractive business proposition. Commercial banks are often unable or unwilling to help such small-scale entrepreneurs. Yet help is available.

It's called micro-credit, and it started in Bangladesh in the 1960s. The idea is to offer small loans to members of the local community, with all proceeds going back into a fund that can then help others. In Bangladesh, 94 percent of the 2.4 million people helped by the Grameen Bank are women who previously had no such opportunity. It goes beyond Asia, too—current estimates suggest that there are 500 million people in poverty worldwide running small businesses that have been backed by micro-credit groups.

These people have the opportunity to make a living. Of course, no one is suggesting that this will solve all of the world's problems in one swoop—poverty is a complex issue—but by supporting groups such as Heed, we are putting our "talent" to good use. Let's not bury it in the ground, but instead, begin to use the resources around us. Our cash, our voice, our prayers—whatever it is, what reason do we have to keep it all to ourselves?

CHAPTER SEVEN

Leaving the Personal Planet

There's a problem with the book of Job. In fact, there are so many problems with this Old Testament book that there are plenty of people who gloss over or ignore it entirely. They may be able to wipe off the mildew in Leviticus and fight their way through the apocalypse in Revelation, but when it comes to Job and the tale of monumental and apparently pointless suffering, some people would rather not bother.

But what should we do with it? Do we give in to the confusion and get bogged down by the bizarre nature of a story seemingly at odds with much of the rest of the Bible? There's the fact that the eponymous hero seems to be more Arab than Jew and that the book contains God's longest speech in the Old Testament—even though the Lord's words amount to little more than a list of rhetorical questions. There's the shocking opening scene where God barters with Satan, along with His seeming allowance of monumental grief to land on Job, for little reason other than to answer the devil's dare. So do we ditch it? Do we accept it as fact, a literal, step-by-step account of God's actions? Can we accept that God could possibly behave in such a way? These are hard questions, but if we turn away from them, we miss the point entirely. The book of Job is a masterpiece, a profoundly significant work that underpins just about everything that is important for anyone trying to find the right way in a life of service of God.

The story is simple. Job lives in Uz, a large territory to the east of the Jordan River. He is quite something, too—wealthy, honest, a good Yahweh-fearing man. There is none greater in all the land, so it's not surprising that God likes him. Typically, having God on your side is considered a good thing, yet when Satan rolls up and starts chatting with God one day, things rapidly turn worse for the family man from Uz. God proclaims that Job is the real deal, a believer with a solid faith. Satan claims otherwise and suggests that Job's allegiance to God will vanish once the going ceases to be so smooth. And so it begins.

Job is hit by four body blows. The Arabs, lightning, the Chaldeans, and a tornado all wreak havoc, destroying his livestock and even his children. He is left stunned, with only his faith intact. What next? He shaves his head. The process of grief might have changed the way he looked, but the verses that follow show that his faith is still there. His words are a truly beautiful submission to God:

"Then he fell to the ground in worship and said: 'Naked I came from my mother's womb, and naked I will depart. The Lord gave and the Lord has taken away; may the name of the Lord be praised.' In all this, Job did not sin by charging God with wrongdoing" (Job 1:20–22).

Then he is afflicted with running sores across his entire body, and his wife suggests that the logical next step might be to curse God. Still he refuses to blame his Maker, even after the arrival of three friends who sit for seven days, silent except for the sounds of their grief. After the week is up, Job has had enough. He finally gives in and curses the day he was born (Job 3:3).

During the ensuing chapters, his friends offer their thoughts on the crisis. Eliphaz reckons Job is suffering because he has sinned; Bildad assumes that Job is in denial, refusing to face up to hidden sin; Zophar goes one step further, suggesting that Job hasn't even gotten half of what he deserves. Eventually Elihu, another friend, speaks up. Elihu's advice is a step up in quality from that of the three musketeers. He seems to have a deeper understanding of the way things are, suggesting that God is a teacher, leading Job on to greater wisdom through his suffering. He also explains why he chose to remain silent for thirty chapters: he was allowing the older and wiser chaps to speak first.

God is not the enemy, and Elihu warns Job about becoming proud of his spiritual endurance. And finally it's over. God's silence is

> **Psalm 140:12**
> I know that the Lord secures justice for the poor and upholds the cause of the needy.

broken with a four-chapter diatribe. But if we were hoping for a clear explanation of why it all happened, we're going to be disappointed. "Brace yourself like a man," Job is told. Strange, perhaps, but the original word used for *man* does not imply a weak man, but a strong one—one ready to fight. God asks him questions, the sort none of us could answer. Job does no better than us, but, standing face to face with God, hearing all that He has done, recognizing once again his place in the universe, Job bows down and worships (Job 42:6). He is restored, has more children, and gets even wealthier. And while the first three chums are told off, Job is held up as a righteous man and lives for many more years.

....

Looking for answers but asking the wrong questions
We make such a hash of the book of Job. We see it through faulty

lenses, getting bogged down with detail that is beside the point. True, the book raises some important questions, the sort that we need to grapple with. After all, it seems to be about the absence of divine justice. God appears removed, acting out of character even at the very start. He simply does not respond when Job asks why he has been made to suffer. How come? Is God embarrassed? Does the Almighty not really know the answer Himself? Then there's the subject of Job's change of heart. Just as Job changes the course he has stuck to so doggedly throughout the story, admitting to God that he was wrong, the Lord breaks radio silence and declares that Job was right after all. Instead, it is the three friends who are reprimanded. So are we to assume that the message of the book is that we should not dare question God? Or should we? Does fate protect, or is it not just? Does God answer us when we call?

To us as readers, the book offers even starker truths. As the main characters search for justice, trying to work out precisely why Job was made to suffer, we know the truth: there was no sin-related reason. He just happened to be the subject of a bizarre experiment between God and Satan. Hardly an enticing prospect, is it?

Traditionally the book has been lumped together with the other wisdom books, Ecclesiastes and Proverbs. Yet there is more to it than is commonly found in those books. There is more fire, a greater revelation of God Himself, that ties it in with a whole other genre of biblical narrative: the prophetic books. Like Malachi, Amos, and Isaiah, it is concerned with the voice of God. It contains God's longest speech in the Old Testament, and what's more, the wisdom books offer advice on how to live a life that does not anger God. Job, on the other hand, gets to stand up and face God like a man.

The story of Job has an appeal that stretches beyond the Church. Sadly, other religions don't seem to do much better when it comes to interpreting the tale correctly. The Marxist literary critics hail him as a hero for being the first to question the authority of God. The feminist critics point to the poor showing that his wife gets and grumble about the misogynistic side of things. There's the greeting-card approach, which sees the whole book as little more than a flimsy response to the presence of suffering, as if to say, "Never mind, at least it's not all that bad, dear."

Most cultures have their own version of the Job story. India's adaptation focuses on the story of the gods and goddesses, wondering whether a single human prince could be found who would be without stain or blemish, as S. Terrien points out:

> Most of the members of the divine assembly were of the opinion that there was none, but Vasishta insisted that a certain Atschandira (Haricandra) was perfect. Shiva Rutren ("the destroyer") offered to prove the contrary if the prince were delivered into his power. Vasishta accepted the challenge and it was agreed that, depending upon the issue of the wager, one would yield to the other all merits acquired in a long series of penance. Shiva Rutren thereupon submitted Atschandira to all sorts of trials, deprived him of his wealth, kingdom, wife and only son, but the prince persisted in his virtue. The gods rewarded him with munificence and returned to him his previous estate. Shiva Rutren gave his own merits to Vasishta, who passed them on to the hero.[1]

The Sumerians, too, writing some two thousand years before the Old Testament was completed, had their own version. Here the sufferer is a man who has been wealthy and good, blessed with family and friends, until one day sickness and adversity overwhelm him. He refuses to condemn his god for allowing such evil, and instead, humbles himself and, with tears, offers prayer and supplication. As a reward for such devotion, the god delivers the man from suffering and restores his well-being. All pretty close to the biblical version, but lacking a certain something. So it is with the Islamic version of the tale, in which Ayyub (the Koran's Job equivalent) is advised to beat his wife for her poor showing on the loyalty front.

Intellectuals have loved the book, even choosing to see it as a comedy, complete with three friends who act the fool and a happy ending to contrast with the chaos of earlier verses. Carl Jung saw Job as depressed, with Satan representing the dark side of his psyche. Shakespeare had a go with *King Lear*, choosing to side with the nihilism, and Beckett's *Waiting for Godot* draws on the shared gene pool—Godot never shows up and the two vagrants finally realize that life itself is futile, that we are "born astride an open grave." The Mormons, however, took a different tack with their 2003 movie *The R.M.*, a comedy about a young man returning from a mission trip to find that everything around him has gone wrong.

Job's hidden jewels

None of these versions quite get it. To focus on the prosperity is to ignore the depth of the suffering; to focus on the suffering is to ignore the remarkable nature of the story. There is a greater message at the heart of the book, one that offers insight into the essential nature of God's gravity.

Job is a model believer. Like Abraham and Amos, he assumed responsibility for righting the wrongs of a fallen society. He was an agent of human justice, and the key was there to be seen in his character. Why was Job chosen? He answered the question himself in chapter 29:

> When I went to the gate of the city and took my seat in the public square, the young men saw me and stepped aside and

the old men rose to their feet; the chief men refrained from speaking and covered their mouths with their hands; the voices of the nobles were hushed, and their tongues stuck to the roof of their mouths. Whoever heard me spoke well of me, and those who saw me commended me, because I rescued the poor who cried for help, and the fatherless who had none to assist them. Those who were dying blessed me; I made the widow's heart sing. I put on righteousness as my clothing; justice was my robe and my turban. I was eyes to the blind and feet to the lame. I was a father to the needy; I took up the case of the stranger. I broke the fangs of the wicked and snatched the victims from their teeth. (Job 29:7–17)

God chose Job not because he was wealthy but because he was upright, a believer whose lifestyle measured up to all his fine words. In a hypothetical scenario where we wonder just how great a believer could be, just how much he could endure, Job is the perfect example, the athlete in ideal condition. His background of defending the weak, serving as an agent of human justice, taking responsibility, doing as Micah suggests—a good deal of walking

WE SHOULD NOT DARE QUESTION GOD? OR SHOULD WE? DOES FATE PROTECT, OR IS IT NOT JUST? DOES GOD ANSWER US WHEN WE CALL?

humbly, loving mercy, and acting justly (Mic. 6:8)—makes him the sort of person who knows the essence of God, as He revealed to Jeremiah:

"'Let not the wise man boast of his wisdom or the strong man boast of his strength or the rich man boast of his riches, but let him who boasts boast about this: that he understands and knows me, that I am the Lord, who exercises kindness, justice and righteousness on earth, for in these I delight,' declares the Lord" (Jer. 9:23–24, NIV).

Job followed the old standards, the classic commandments that Jesus returned to (see Matthew 22:37, Mark 12:30, Luke 10:27): that you "love the Lord your God with all your heart and with all your soul and with all your strength" (Deut. 6:5) and "do not seek revenge or bear a grudge against any one among your people, but love your neighbor as yourself" (Lev. 19:18). By putting self behind service, others in front of personal needs, Job had earned the right to be singled out by God.

There is another reason behind Job's status as a model believer, besides his dedication to Christ's virtues of service and sacrifice: he was rock-solid in his devotion to God. After telling Job to brace himself like a man, to prepare for a fight, God asked him questions, the sort none of us could answer. Job ultimately did what was good and right—and just about the only decent thing to do: he got down and worshiped God. The greatest of all believers, face-down in the dirt.

Job: fact or fiction?

It is hard to believe that the story of Job is a factual account of a real-life story. Surely the book is an allegory, a story with profound symbolic meaning. Tennyson called it "the greatest poem of ancient and modern times," and it makes sense to see it as such. After all, if we don't see it as fiction, if it really did happen, then we are faced with the prospect that perhaps God is decidedly crueler than we first thought. He ends up being one of those "wanton boys" who spend their time picking the wings off flies, just as the blinded character Gloucester accuses Him in *King Lear*. So instead of being a description of real events, the book of Job works far better as a blueprint, a set of plans, for the attitudes that God holds dear. We are supposed to be like Job, even if God is not quite like the God we see in the story.

If this is an allegory, what does it represent? Some people believe that it could have been written by Isaiah, and it's true that there are elements of God's bragging to Satan that remind us of Hezekiah's bragging to the Babylonians (which we looked at in the last chapter). Isaiah criticized Hezekiah after that incident. Perhaps the prophet was using Job's story as a means of reflecting on Hezekiah's life. Hezekiah became ill (like Job) and ultimately saw Judah annexed and brutally conquered, handed over to the Babylonians. Like Job, he lost a great deal. And like Job, his fall seemed unjust, as if God had withdrawn from His people without good reason.

At the end of Job we find out that our hero's fortunes are restored. Is this what the Israelites hoped for? David Wolfers suggests that we take a close look at precisely how this happens:

"After Job had prayed for his friends, the Lord made him prosperous again" (Job 42:10, NIV).

The two halves of the sentence are clearly linked. When Job offers forgiveness and compassion to those who have blighted his life for so long, things suddenly return to their previous state. Wolfers suggests that the book is therefore a lesson the Israelites need to learn—to open up their minds and start doling out compassion to a wider range of people.[2] Perhaps this is the prompt they need to start seeing Yahweh as not only the God of Abraham, but the God of the Gentiles, too.

If the allegory worked for the audience of that day, could it have a similar application for us today? Is there any need for us to hear the call for reconciliation? Do we need to learn to do a little better at breaking out of our narrow ideas about whom God likes? Do we need to hand out a little more forgiveness to those who have done us wrong?

HIS LOVE OF GOD MEANT THAT HE STUCK CLOSE TO HIS BELIEFS, REGARDLESS OF THE TORMENT HE ENDURED.

But that still leaves the problem of why God would choose to represent Himself as silent, evasive, cruel, and unpredictable. Perhaps the book is not a revelation of how God sees Himself, but rather an attempt by man to explain God, to wonder why the plot may not be going according to our plans.

Does this alter our opinion of the book? Is it somehow less impressive to consider this as a flawed or unreliable depiction of God? Some might be tempted to downgrade the book's worth. But whoever wrote this—and it must have been a brilliant person, with knowledge of astronomy, zoology, and legal procedure—is surely reflecting on a revelation of God's priorities. Surely the book of Job tells us more about how we respond to God and others than about how God treats His creation. Job is celebrated for his devotion and integrity; his love of justice and acceptance of responsibility mark him as the most remarkable of all.

His love of God meant that he stuck close to his beliefs, regardless of the torment he endured. These are the marks of a person drawn in by God's gravity—humility, obedience, and a willingness to serve others and to love God, whatever the storms.

Jonathan Sacks draws the links between Job's suffering and success:

"Faith does not mean certainty. It means the courage to live with uncertainty. It does not mean answers; it means asking questions, it means that the challenge has not been sent as a punishment, but as a call to responsibility."[3]

He is right. What counts is our determination to adopt an active faith, not a passive one. Like Job and Abraham and Amos, we need to stand up and question the presence of things that are wrong in the world around us. Job pondered whether misfortune was always the result of sin. Three of his friends declared that it was; one said that it was not. God, in the end, did not answer; He simply told Job to stand up, face the Almighty, and ask the questions.

The Jews had no significant belief in life after death, believing instead in She'ol, a shadow-style underworld. To them, reward and punishment were to be found and handled in this life alone. In chapter 3 Job feels that She'ol is close, that "shadow and deep darkness" would override the day of his birth. The Hebrew root of the word is *sha'al*, meaning "to ask, to question, to interrogate." Job may have felt as if his time was slipping away, yet in reality he was on the path toward asking questions of God and finally receiving answers.

Closing thoughts ...

Where does the idea of God's gravity fit into the book of Job? It reminds us of the true jewels of relationship with God: the determination to remain devoted, whatever the weather; the act of supporting, nurturing, protecting, and providing for those whose lives have been scarred as a consequence of a fallen world; the responsibility we have to submit to the mandate to love and serve God and others. We must be prepared to act justly, to love mercy, to walk humbly with our God, just as Micah instructed.

We've spent a while chewing on the concepts, exploring the ideas, and wondering about the way in which we can turn the tables on a me-first faith. And talk is good, but it only lasts so long. There comes a point when we need to move. Like Job, we need to stand up and break the silence; like Abraham, we need to step up to the challenge; like Esther, we need to take the risk; like Moses, we need to make ourselves available; like Amos, we need to begin to right the wrongs that surround us. It's time to let go of the railing and see where God's gravity might pull us. It's time to act—almost.

CHASING FREEDOM

....

For a capital city, Freetown has an odd name. It sounds a bit too unreal, as if it were plucked out of a hat filled with competition entries. But for its inhabitants, as well as the rest of those living in Sierra Leone, life over the past twelve years has been very real indeed. Eighteen-year-old Fatmata knows this all too well.

Fatmata, a hairdresser, lives and works in a tiny tarpaulin tent at the entrance of the Freetown amputee camp. She's lived there for the last four years, ever since fighters from the Revolutionary United Front (RUF) made her an orphan. One day her father and sister were killed, her mother disappeared, and her foot was cut off as "a message to the president."

Later, West African peacekeepers found her and took her to the hospital, but it was too late to save her leg.

Afterward, she moved to the amputee camp and became a Christian through the loving support of other Christians there. Even though Fatmata has done the incomprehensible—believed in God despite such meaningless suffering—the anguish of her memories is raw.

....

THE PAST

Fatmata is not alone. During its eleven-year civil war, Sierra Leone lost sons and daughters by the thousands, whole families and generations were wiped out, and villages were destroyed as the government fought the foot soldiers for control of one of the country's most valuable commodities: diamonds. The RUF responded to a slogan used by the government—"Hands Up for Peace"—by amputating limbs or burning their RUF initials into people's arms. It is estimated that fifty thousand people died in the conflicts, while a significant number were forced to flee their homes.[4]

> The Bible is filled with examples of forgiveness. Time after time, God welcomes back sinners. Yet one example in particular stands out: Jesus on the cross. Why? Because it cost Him dearly (Matt. 26:39, 27:46) and was so important that as one of His final acts, He forgave (Luke 23:34). Forgiveness is difficult. But it is also essential.

But it's easy to get lost in the figures. It's also tempting to imagine that life in Sierra Leone now is anything but "free." Yet the truth is different. Thanks to the remarkable courage of the people, the tireless work of Christian groups, and the grace and mercy of God Himself, there is a new hope dawning.

THE PRESENT

The people of Sierra Leone need all kinds of tools, from the ones that will allow them to feed themselves to those that will bring harmony and forgiveness. To give people hope for the future, Tearfund partner Evangelical Fellowship of Sierra Leone (EFSL) works among rural communities, distributing seeds and tools to farmers, repairing wells, and running peace-building workshops. These workshops teach people how to forgive their enemies and put the past behind them.

Margaret Conteh of EFSL knows just how important this is. "Revenge will not allow your arm or leg to grow again," she says. "So forgive and let love into your heart."

Yet Margaret is no ivory-tower outsider. When she speaks of the need for forgiveness, it comes from her own experience. When she listens to stories of pain and suffering, she has her own to remember.

As the fighting escalated, she and her family were forced to flee their home. "We ran from village to village," she says. "Sometimes there'd be no room for us, and we'd sleep on the floor of a kitchen or bathroom. You could feel the war. It pinched you in your bones."

THE FUTURE

It is impossible to think about the war in Sierra Leone without feeling a sense of horror at the scale of human suffering. It is also impossible to look at the way the people are moving forward without feeling massively humbled by their compassion and bravery.

Take Abu, for example. He was a two-month-old baby being held by his father when rebels entered their village and opened fire. One of the bullets ripped through Abu's leg. His dad was killed immediately.

His mother, Kadiatu, managed to escape with her four other children. She thought Abu was dead, and is certain that it is only by the grace of God that he is still alive. After her little boy was released from the hospital, they moved to the amputee camp in Freetown, where Abu is living, running around with the help of an artificial limb. Kadiatu became a Christian through the love and support of others in the camp.

No one is suggesting that the future is easy for people like Adu, his mom, and Fatmata, but Freetown might not be such an odd name after all.

CHAPTER EIGHT

Giving In to the Pull

So what does it mean to give in to the pull of God's gravity? What difference will it make in the daily rhythm of our lives if we choose to reject the practice of placing ourselves at the center of the universe? The truth is that as we opt to pursue a more God-centered way of life, our daily actions should bear the fruits as we become more selfless, obedient, just, sacrificial, and compassionate. We will find ourselves pulled in toward our Creator, seeing every aspect of our lives challenged, never arriving at that final destination where our human forms can sit back and relax, having finally reached the required levels of sacrificial living. It will affect how we pray, fast, study, and relate to God one on one. It will impact our choices made as individuals, from shopping to career aspirations, finance to travel. We will find ourselves compelled to be a part of active, progressive communities, whether political, local, social, or international. We will not keep quiet, but will quietly change the worlds around us, starting with our own.

We've spent much of the book looking at the way in which our attitudes and aspirations can wander off course, the way we easily become distracted by things that are beside the point. We've talked about money, about retreating from the less-than-glossy aspects of God's challenge, about using the satisfaction of our own egos as fuel for our actions. We've looked at the way we pull away from God's gravity. Is there time enough for us to wonder how to get pulled in? The rest of the book offers some concrete, practical challenges to the day-to-day aspects of our lives—issues on which we can, and should, be making a difference. Yet at the heart of all our worthy work and good intentions must come one simple yet profoundly important thing: our relationship with God. Without it, our struggles to offer human justice miss the essential point in life—that we were created to love, live alongside, and follow God. Anything less is second-best.

The Old Testament prophet Micah understood this. A contemporary of Isaiah, Micah stood a little closer to the farmer Amos than the well-connected headline prophet. Micah came from the wrong side of town—a rural border town, unimpressive and close to the dangerous Philistine territory of Gath. His book has a fierce political bite to it, taking up the struggle of the oppressed, fighting for the rights of those too easily forgotten. Where Isaiah, the resident of Jerusalem, sees the bigger political picture, Micah's message is more like the word on the street.

Early on in his book he criticizes the leaders, accusing them of treating their subjects like pieces of meat, prey from whom the flesh can easily be ripped. Later the priests and quality religious types are given a rough ride and told off for their narrow worldview. It seems that they were prepared to switch allegiance, so long as their stomachs remained full. Throughout the book it is clear that the abuse of power is considered worthy of God's judgment.

The killer line comes in chapter 6: "And what does the Lord require of you? To act justly and to love mercy and to walk humbly with your God" (Mic. 6:8).

It's a good verse too, but one that can easily be confused. After all, we could religiously apply these three instructions to life and still end up completely missing the point about Christianity. To get the full picture, we need to understand the context of the verse. Not a lot of context, either—just the seven verses that come before it. Together they form a long list of Israel's skills at making religious offerings. Yet these skills alone are not enough. What Micah makes clear is that the Israelites need to go beyond the verbal expression of devotion and give it a decidedly practical edge. They need to develop an outwardly active faith to accompany the inward devotion.

In other words, a true faith in God, a life lived according to the correct order of things, will be both worshipful and just. It will express devotion through song and sacrifice, within and without the walls of the

"Don't waste life in doubts and fears; spend yourself on the work before you, well assured that the right performance of this hour's duties will be the best preparation for the hours and ages that will follow it."
—Ralph Waldo Emerson

Church. It makes sense that we ought to develop something of an allergic reaction to the presence of injustice, to love and long for kindness in all relationships, whether with family, colleagues, state, strangers, or God. When we act out of humility and recognize that we are utterly dependent on God for all things, our fine words and highest praise will become entwined with the very acts that Micah's words pull into focus. Our devotion and lifestyle will place God at the heart of the matter. Not us, or even others. Just God.

Why did Jesus have to die?

We like to have a plan. We like to be able to follow a multi-point strategy for changing whatever it is that needs to be changed around us. Whether it is falling church attendance or increasing waistlines, it helps to have an ABC to Making Things Better. Or at least it appears to help. But our faith is not about a plan or a system, no matter how comforting they may be. Yes, God's gravity draws us closer to justice and mercy and social change, and yes, we can even measure these things, pointing to the lives of fellow believers who have gone before and left a trail of social transformation in their wake. Most importantly, however, God's gravity pulls us closer to Him. Engagement, relationship, and responsibility are so vital to our time here on earth that God's Son even endured the agony of the cross in order to restore the wayward balance.

Understanding the death of Jesus allows us to construct a framework for faith on which to build a solid relationship with God. Theologian N. T. Wright walks the reader through the story with skill in *The Challenge of Jesus*, starting off by encouraging us to cast our eyes back to Genesis.[1]

> Then the man and his wife heard the sound of the Lord God as he was walking in the garden in the cool of the day, and they hid from the Lord God among the trees of the garden. But the Lord God called to the man, "Where are you?" He answered, "I heard you in the garden, and I was afraid because I was naked; so I hid." And he said, "Who told you that you were naked? Have you eaten from the tree that I commanded you not to eat from?" The man said, "The woman you put here with me—she gave me some fruit from the tree, and I ate it." Then the Lord God said to the woman, "What is this you have done?" The woman said, "The serpent deceived me, and I ate." (Gen. 3:8–13).

This is the first, but not the last, depiction of humans sinning. In this case, however, the act itself is relatively tame—just a bite or two from an apple. Yet of course, the issue has nothing to do with the fruit, but with the disobedience exhibited by the plucking and the munching. We can assume that the serpent was not concerned with the dietary needs of the first couple. No, it wanted to bring separation between man and God. And it nearly worked. After the incident, the couple was banished from the strolling ground, and the parameters of the relationship changed dramatically for the worse. God simply cannot have sin around. It's not that He doesn't like it or finds it mildly irritating. He simply cannot have it around.

We get a glimpse of God's attitude toward sin on the eve of the Israelite's miraculous escape, in His careful preparation for judgement on the oppressive Egyptian regime.

> The Lord said to Moses and Aaron in Egypt, "This month
> is to be for you the first month, the first month of your
> year. Tell the whole community of Israel that on the tenth
> day of this month each man is to take a lamb for his family,
> one for each household. If any household is too small
> for a whole lamb, they must share one with their nearest
> neighbor, having taken into account the number of people
> there are. You are to determine the amount of lamb needed
> in accordance with what each person will eat. The animals
> you choose must be year-old males without defect, and you
> may take them from the sheep or the goats. Take care of
> them until the fourteenth day of the month, when all the
> members of the community of Israel must slaughter them at
> twilight. Then they are to take some of the blood and put it
> on the sides and tops of the doorframes of the houses where
> they eat the lambs. That same night they are to eat the meat
> roasted over the fire, along with bitter herbs, and bread made
> without yeast. Do not eat the meat raw or boiled in water,

but roast it over a fire—with the head, legs and internal organs. Do not leave any of it till morning; if some is left till morning, you must burn it. This is how you are to eat it: with your cloak tucked into your belt, your sandals on your feet and your staff in your hand. Eat it in haste; it is the Lord's Passover. On that same night I will pass through Egypt and strike down every firstborn of both people and animals, and I will bring judgment on all the gods of Egypt. I am the Lord. The blood will be a sign for you on the houses where you are, and when I see the blood, I will pass over you. No destructive plague will touch you when I strike Egypt." (Exod. 12:1–13)

The instructions God gave were full of meaning, like the fact that the lamb or kid was to be a perfect year-old male—much more expensive than a female. Its blood loss was to be a token of sacrifice, one that God would recognize. That it was to be completely consumed showed that the whole animal was to be considered part of the sacrifice.

SIN—WHETHER INTENTIONAL OR NOT—NEEDS TO BE PAID FOR.

God's judgment was upon a whole group of people who had done wrong. For others—for His own people—these instructions were the way to avoid that judgment. Only something costly could pay the price; what's more, only those who obeyed His instructions would know how to prepare themselves. God told them to always remember this Passover. Far more than just an empty ritual, the act forced the participant to remember the power, the protection, and the perfection that surrounds God.

After the escape and the Red Sea and the drama that followed, Moses was yet again the chosen vehicle for God's education of the masses:

The Lord said to Moses, "Say to the Israelites: 'When anyone
sins unintentionally and does what is forbidden in any of
the Lord's commands—If the anointed priest sins, bringing
guilt on the people, he must bring to the Lord a young bull
without defect as a sin offering for the sin he has committed
... If a member of the community sins unintentionally and
does what is forbidden in any of the Lord's commands, he
is guilty. When he is made aware of the sin he committed,
he must bring as his offering for the sin he committed a
female goat without defect. He is to lay his hand on the
head of the sin offering and slaughter it at the place of the
burnt offering. Then the priest is to take some of the blood
with his finger and put it on the horns of the altar of burnt
offering and pour out the rest of the blood at the base of the
altar. He shall remove all the fat, just as the fat is removed
from the fellowship offering, and the priest shall burn it on
the altar as an aroma pleasing to the Lord. In this way the
priest will make atonement for him, and he will be forgiven.
If he brings a lamb as his sin offering, he is to bring a
female without defect. He is to lay his hand on its head and
slaughter it for a sin offering at the place where the burnt
offering is slaughtered. Then the priest shall take some of the
blood of the sin offering with his finger and put it on the
horns of the altar of burnt offering and pour out the rest of
the blood at the base of the altar. He shall remove all the fat,
just as the fat is removed from the lamb of the fellowship
offering, and the priest shall burn it on the altar on top of
the offerings made to the Lord by fire. In this way the priest
will make atonement for him for the sin he has committed,
and he will be forgiven.'" (Lev. 4:1–3, 27–35, NIV)

The rules are not so much about the imposition of rules for the mere
sake of it; instead, they are God's way of caring for His people. He
has given them guidelines about how to behave well, but now He

details how they should act when their behavior is less than ideal. Sin—whether intentional or not—needs to be paid for. Back in those days the currency was sacrificial offerings, and there was a whole load of them to choose from. The burnt, grain, and fellowship offerings were optional, but the sin and guilt offerings had to be done—there was simply no getting away from it.

But why? God was after the hearts of His people, and this complex set of rituals was designed with one purpose in mind: to remind them of all that He had done for them. In making sacrifices expensive, He was yet again sending a clear message that sin does not go without consequences; it demands payment.

Isaiah starts to provide the links between the Old and the New Testaments:

> Who has believed our message and to whom has the arm of the Lord been revealed? He grew up before him like a tender shoot, and like a root out of dry ground. He had no beauty or majesty to attract us to him, nothing in his appearance that we should desire him. He was despised and rejected by others, a man of suffering and familiar with pain. Like one from whom people hide their faces he was despised, and we held him in low esteem. Surely he took up our pain and bore our suffering, yet we considered him punished by God, stricken by him, and afflicted. But he was pierced for our transgressions, he was crushed for our iniquities; the punishment that brought us peace was on him, and by his wounds we are healed. We all, like sheep, have gone astray, each of us has turned to our own way; and the Lord has laid on him the iniquity of us all. He was oppressed and afflicted, yet he did not open his mouth; he was led like a lamb to the slaughter, and as a sheep before its shearers is silent, so he did not open his mouth. By

oppression and judgment he was taken away. Yet who of
his generation protested? For he was cut off from the land
of the living; for the transgression of my people he was
punished. He was assigned a grave with the wicked, and
with the rich in his death, though he had done no violence,
nor was any deceit in his mouth. (Isa. 53:1–9)

This whole chapter is a vital player in the Bible. Parts of it get quoted
in the New Testament (in Matthew, John, and Romans, to name
but three), and it presents us with the clearest explanation of sin and
atonement. This poem of Isaiah's is at the heart of his book and points
to the life of Jesus, to the salvation of His people. It was intended to
be relevant to Isaiah's contemporaries, but the truths echo across the
centuries—like the fact that the Messiah comes not because He's
bored or lonely, but because we need Him; He comes for "our pain
... our suffering." It's foolish for us to think that He deserved what
happened; He wasn't "punished by God." The truth is harder for us to
bear, but we must accept it: "he was crushed for our iniquities"—for
our sin, our wrongdoing, our straying from His laws. We accumulated
the bill, and He was the One who paid. What's more, that payment
bought something utterly special: peace, healing, and salvation. But
there's even more to say, and Isaiah puts it brilliantly: we're all guilty;
"we all, like sheep, have gone astray" and are in debt to God. Read
through Isaiah 53 slowly, carefully, and it's impossible to deny the
links between our sin and Jesus' suffering, between His sacrifice and
our salvation.

Paul's knowledge of the ancient Scriptures is clear when we read his
letter to the church in Rome:

You see, at just the right time, when we were still powerless,
Christ died for the ungodly. Very rarely will anyone die for a
righteous person, though for a good person someone might
possibly dare to die. But God demonstrates his own love

for us in this: While we were still sinners, Christ died for us.
Since we have now been justified by his blood, how much
more shall we be saved from God's wrath through him! For
if, while we were God's enemies, we were reconciled to
him through the death of his Son, how much more, having
been reconciled, shall we be saved through his life! Not only
is this so, but we also boast in God through our Lord Jesus
Christ, through whom we have now received reconciliation.
(Rom. 5:6–11)

THE HARD BIT COMES WHEN WE ASK WHETHER WE REALLY WERE GOD'S ENEMIES.

—

The links and parallels
between this passage
and Isaiah 53 are
clear: we are all
sinners; Jesus died for
us; His blood paid the
price, bringing us out
of exile and home to God. It is through not only Jesus' death but His
resurrection that we can now have some kind of intimate relationship
with God, secure in the knowledge that the debt has been paid, that
the guilt and sin have been dealt with.

The hard bit comes when we ask whether we really were God's
enemies. Though it may seem a tad harsh, the strength of the words
does nothing to undermine their truth. Unbelief is hostility; choosing
to reject God places us opposite Him. However, it was Jesus' actions,
so motivated by love, that made the first move. While we were against
Him, His death put things right. As Leviticus illumines, sin demands
payment in order to be wiped out. Romans 5:11 makes it clear:
Jesus has bought us back, made the ultimate exchange, and prepared
the way for us to approach God. Can we really ignore such reckless
generosity?

"While he was still speaking, Judas, one of the Twelve, arrived. With him was a large crowd armed with swords and clubs, sent from the chief priests and the elders of the people. Now the betrayer had arranged a signal with them: 'The one I kiss is the man; arrest him.' Going at once to Jesus, Judas said, 'Greetings, Rabbi!' and kissed him. Jesus replied, 'Friend, do what you came for'" (Matt. 26:47–50).

Discussing the death of Jesus in terms of its symbolic meaning—that He died to pay the price, to give us life, and so on—is important, but we risk ignoring the other, more physical reasons for Christ's death: He died because His friend betrayed Him. He died because He had enemies in high places. He was a victim of complex politics. He was let down by the crowd. Jesus died because He was a man, and as we can see in the world around us, bad things happen to good people. Tragedy happens.

Jesus' death was not a mistake, nor was He unlucky or unwise to end up on the cross. Could He have taken another path and lived out His days in gentle comfort as a good man with an aging smile? No. Jesus was always going to die. It was part of the plan, part of the route toward our salvation. In choosing to come to earth, Jesus chose the ending on the cross. And that is where the power comes: because He was a willing, living, perfect sacrifice, Jesus' death was worth more than all the year-old lambs that would ever exist. This extravagant, painful, agonizing, confounding end to His life bears all the hallmarks of a parent who longs for his or her estranged and endangered child to return.

Originally we were made to stand face to face with God. Death may seem unnatural, but relationship is deep within the core of each of us. We see it in our reproduction and in the way that a nursing mother nurtures new life, where eyes connect and ties deeper than words could ever express are formed. Relationship is everything. Formula is nothing.

So when we give in to the pull of God's gravity, we are giving in to God. We are not following a program or relying on a routine. Such things are not the way of relationships. Programs and routines had little place on the cross, and they have little to offer us that is of benefit today. Instead of trusting in our own ability to stick to a three-point plan of faith, we must allow our attitudes to be shaped by God rather than by our own desires. Then we will see that we make a choice for relationship instead of isolation. Just as Jesus turned the world upside down with His outwardly focused life, so too must we look beyond our own isolated borders and engage in the very relationship with our Creator for which we were first made.

A thought about relating to God

Faith can be hard. Like all relationships, particularly the ones carried out over long distances, the difficulties of communication can threaten to overwhelm us. But if we choose to reduce our belief in God to a set of rules, or if we turn our backs on Him altogether, we miss the point entirely. Our legalism and lawlessness may offer the promise of both comfort and security—that if we follow the rules we will make it through the maze, that if we serve ourselves alone we will end up ultimately satisfied—yet both are doomed, for precisely the same reason: they take us away from relationship with God. They move us further out from the divine event horizon, out to a colder, staler place.

Legalism and lawlessness creep in with guile and cunning, yet true relationship with God clears a path through the mess. The life of Christ personifies freedom, making it perfectly clear how well the flesh of faith hangs on the bones of God's commandments. The Israelites struggled throughout history to live up to His commands, no matter how clearly they were told to get on track. Like the rest of us, they chose to orbit their own desires, fears, and interests instead of God's. Part of Jesus' genius was that He transformed what appeared (on the evidence of generations of the chosen people) to be an unworkable system. Where God's people allowed their hearts to wander and their ethics to become cloudy, Jesus was the perfect embodiment of God's two great commands—to love God with all that we have and to love others as much as we love ourselves. With roots in the earliest texts that guided the Israelites' path, the words of Christ remain as relevant to us today as they did two thousand years ago, encouraging us to pursue a thoroughly selfless, outwardly focused type of obedience and sacrifice.

Three problems to consider

Our task is not to be Jesus. We are not equal partners with God, not a pair of hands essential to His work. The truth is far less grand: we are His creation, His people made for His glory—made to know Him, trust Him, and love Him, allowing His love and care to, in turn, take full root in our lives. Our job is not to impress God with our acts of service any more than it is to turn Him on with our culturally exciting

> **Psalm 112:5**
> Good will come to those who are generous and lend freely, who conduct their affairs with justice.

worship. Our aim is not to become self-consciously holy, running through a ritual of religious virtue. We are made to have relationship with our heavenly Father. Nothing less.

God's gravity pulls us toward the Father and away from our own small-minded, safe, and vain worlds. It pulls us toward His values and, in doing so, often distances us from the values held up by so many others. And in drawing us closer to Him, we cannot fail to share God's values, joining Him in the grief, sorrow, and anger that is sparked as we view the world around us.

Like poverty. With more than one billion of our fellow men, women, and children living on less than $1 a day—20 percent of the total population—our world is a mess. In Africa the poverty rate is on the rise, with a staggering 46.4 percent of the population failing to hit the $1-per-day mark. For these people, average income has slipped in recent years, now reaching as little as $0.60 per day. More than 25 percent of all children in the developing world are malnourished, and we see thirty thousand children die every twenty-four hours simply because of the severe hardship that comes with extreme poverty and vulnerability to preventable diseases. Slum-dwelling increased in southern Asia between 1990 and 2001, as it has in East Asia, sub-Saharan Africa, Latin America—everywhere, in fact, except North Africa.[2]

Like injustice. Simple diseases like measles are easily vaccinated against—routinely so in the developed world—yet in 2002 the disease claimed the lives of 540,000 children. A woman in labor is sixty-two times more likely to die if giving birth in Africa than in the developed world. In some African countries more than a quarter of adults are HIV-positive, while across sub-Saharan Africa, 57 percent of those infected are women. Young women are increasingly vulnerable to the spread of AIDS, something that is fueled by a mixture of misogyny, patriarchal values, and a refusal to change in response to the current chaos. Antiretroviral therapy is essential yet too often withheld, while basic awareness about prevention is simply not getting through. The number of AIDS orphans is on the rise; twelve million in Africa have lost one parent to the disease, while four million have lost both. Within five years this number is set to rise to 18.4 million. Today there are as many as fifteen million AIDS orphans worldwide.[3]

Like the environment. The organic kiwi fruit that graced my
porridge this morning created more than eight times its weight in
carbon dioxide while in transport to the United Kingdom from
New Zealand,[4] while scientists at the University of Wisconsin predict
that in future years, the least wealthy countries with the lowest
greenhouse gas emissions will find themselves the most vulnerable to
the realities of climate change. The numbers of deaths from malaria,
diarrheal diseases, and malnutrition will double by 2030,[5] due simply
to the fact that our
world is warming.
The latest predictions
forecast that by 2050,
current crop yields
will have to double
in order to keep
pace with increasing
populations. The

**A WOMAN IN LABOR IS SIXTY-TWO
TIMES MORE LIKELY TO DIE IF
GIVING BIRTH IN AFRICA THAN IN
THE DEVELOPED WORLD.**

trouble is that the high levels of CO_2 predicted for 2050 will more
than likely cause crop yields to fall by 50 percent.[6] On our watch
the world has continued to march toward a threat that has the power
to pour chaos and suffering on millions. Yet we have remained
ineffective in challenging the forces that ravage the earth. In the
twelve years from 1990 to 2002, the developed world failed to
reduce its CO_2 emissions.[7] As Pan Yue, deputy director of the state
environmental protection agency in China, puts it, "Environmental
crisis is no longer a risk we predict for our children; it is a problem
that our generation must face. It is going to hit us in fifteen years, not
fifty."[8]

What are we going to do? We need to take it personally. We need to
understand God's concerns well enough to know that this current
state of affairs is horrendous, a set of failing values that Amos, Micah,
and Isaiah would clearly have spoken out against. We need to turn
the tables on our me-first faith enough to know that God's passion

for justice and mercy is rivaled only by His call for obedience and sacrifice from those who claim to love and follow Him.

Do we need to be convinced that God has a problem with poverty? Trotting out a series of verses makes our faith into something more like Bible bingo than a relationship with the Creator, God Almighty. If we cannot see that poverty and oppression and abuse are contrary to God's plan, if we refuse to sign up to the argument that places us as agents of change directly opposite the forces of oppression, then something is wrong. Without justice, without God's people charging ahead to act as agents of human justice, we are not much better than the objects of Amos' scorn. You may not agree with the interpretation of Matthew 25 that suggests that unless we clothe the naked, feed the hungry, and uphold the rights of the oppressed, our salvation is under question. Even so, without justice, the Bible is empty. Without God acting to right the wrongs of a fallen world, the Word fails the world. Without God's people driven to act as agents of human justice out of obedience and sacrifice to God, the world is silent. Inability to appreciate the importance of our active participation in alleviating poverty, tackling oppression, or righting the wrongs of a selfish world is not an excuse for inaction. It should be a cause for repentance and a spur for change.

Nothing is written

Can we change? Can we alter our course and head back toward the pull of our Creator, a force so very at odds with many of the others at work upon our lives? In the 1962 film *Lawrence of Arabia*, there is a sequence in which English soldier T.E. Lawrence (played by Peter O'Toole) takes a band of fifty Arabs to capture the Turkish garrison at the port of Aqaba. His plan relies on the element of surprise gained by crossing the brutally hot Nefud Desert. Sherif Ali (Omar Sharif) questions the wisdom of such a decision:

Sherif: From here until we reach the other side, no water but what we carry with us. For the camels, no water at all. If the camels die, we die. And in twenty days they will start to die.

Lawrence: There's no time to waste then, is there?

The Arabian Desert is immense, the crossing a challenge to mind and body. In the midst of the scalding heat, dust storms, and swirling cyclones, the trek exhausts and kills some of the men. As they reach the end of the desert, it becomes clear that one of their number—Gasim—is not on his camel. Lawrence immediately insists on returning to find him:

Sherif: In God's name, understand: we cannot go back.
Lawrence: I can ...
Sherif: If you go back, you'll kill us all. Gasim you have killed already.
Lawrence: Get out of my way.
Another Arab: Gasim's time is come, Lawrence. It is written!
Lawrence: Nothing is written.
Sherif (riding back with Lawrence): Go back, then. What did you bring us here for with your blasphemous conceit? Eh, English blasphemer? Aqaba? What is Aqaba? You will not be at Aqaba, English. Go back, blasphemer! But you will not be at Aqaba!
Lawrence (riding ahead and turning): I shall be at Aqaba. That is written ... (He points at his head) ... in here!
Sherif (shouting after him): English! English!

The scene that follows is triumphant. Lawrence retraces his steps; finds the half-dead Gasim, delirious with exhaustion; rescues him; and returns to the oasis camp with Gasim clinging to his saddle. Surrounded by curious, grateful, and stunned men who never expected his return, Lawrence fixes a piercing, blazing look on Sherif Ali. Before drinking the water offered to him, he defiantly and proudly repeats his earlier mantra. Rasping, his voice cracks out the words: "Nothing is written."

Is change possible? Nothing is written. Can we shrug off the baggage and bulk of a culture that propels us toward our own desires? Of course we can. The Bible itself is a testimony of the power of man to turn away from God, only to find that God's power to welcome him back outweighs even the most selfish of hearts. It is in the life of Jesus that we see, more clearly than in any other example, how a life will look when pulled in by God's gravity. Selfless, obedient, sacrificial, eternal, generous, dedicated, just, brave, humble. The path is clear.

Instead of the theorizing that surrounds black holes and other contemporary astronomical theories, God's gravity works on principles that are simple enough for all to understand. It will see us take on responsibility, asking questions of a world spinning out of control. Like Abraham, Amos, and Moses, we will speak out against that which appears wrong, taking personally the plight of others. We will become passionate about the presence of human justice, not merely passive spectators channel-surfing in the hope that God might hand out some of the more divine variety. We will become aware of the importance of an outwardly active faith. The days of self-indulgent introspection will appear gray and lifeless. Instead, our beliefs will propel us to physically stand, sit, weep, kneel, and walk alongside those whose fortunes place them at the very top of God's agenda. Our desire for comfort will push us closer to God than to material possessions. We will refuse to be fooled by the veil of ignorance that suggests we can consume without giving a thought to how that affects the lives of others. We might feel like recreating our own Eden, retreating to a place of apparent safety—whether it's the ghetto of Christian culture or a life where God remains locked in a box of our own making—but the temptation will set off the alarm. Instead, we will take risks; we will get involved; we will turn tables, starting with those cluttering up our own lives. We will see all these things as the logical, natural, vital outcome of an intimate faith, a relevant relationship with God. Standing outside empty tombs, we will feel a mixture of grief and thanks, of pain and joy, for death won't define us and grief won't overwhelm us. Thanksgiving will find its way to our lips because we will know our place in the care of a loving, powerful, just Father.

Put this way, the prospect threatens to overawe. Perhaps it excites even more, but the change ahead of us is monumental. And the key is simple. It can be found in the small steps. We may even have been trying out a few already—forgiving, trusting, giving away, writing, campaigning, discussing, rejecting—but however far we have or have not come, the next year, week, or twenty-four hours are an as-yet unplanned journey for us all. Which direction are we going to travel? Toward self or toward God? Internally indulgent or outwardly active? We can start this small journey right now, with a choice to change, a desire to do something different, no matter how seemingly small or insignificant. Arriving at the destination is, for now, irrelevant. What matters is our direction, our decision to let go of the railing and allow ourselves to be pulled in by a force more powerful than any we can imagine. Nothing is impossible. Nothing is written.

PART 2

Enough of the theory, it's time for action. Over the next few pages we're going to be looking at clothes, finances, and the environment. Why? Because they're part of the everyday domino effect that our lifestyle has on others. But this is no fashion show blended with bank managers and biology teachers. Instead, it's about facing up to the impact that many of our current lifestyle choices have on much of the rest of the world. It's about acknowledging mistakes and finding ways to put things right. It's about rolling out the human justice and giving in to God's gravity.

One more thing—this is just a start. It's not a formula for perfection, but a way to look at some issues that might work for you as a model for examining other parts of your life. More than anything, though, this is a small step, a chance to put faith into action, to give our fine words of worship the bite of integrity, the opportunity to get closer to God by doing what we were made for. You'll go further than this—you may even have gotten a lot of the issues sorted out already—but the act of breaking out of a me-first faith will always bring you face to face with the reality of a simple choice: self-service or self-sacrifice.

Finally, there's so much more to say about all this than you'll find in this book, and most of it needs to be said by you. Take a trip to *www. godsgravity.com* and see the stories unfold.

CHAPTER NINE

What Do Our Clothes Say About Us?

I have several fears that are stored away in the blast-proof bunker of my subconscious. One of them is getting wheeled into a crowded social function while naked in bed—but that's not quite so relevant to our topic. The fear I'm thinking of is this: changing rooms. Those little places where you have so little time, light, and space to make up your mind about a garment. They freak me out. Why? Well, things have never been the same since I was eleven. There I was, half-naked and humiliated, wearing a polka-dot tutu as my mom made me try on dresses for my cousin Lisa's birthday present because she said we were the same build. It's not much better these days, either—thanks to the aid of seventeen different mirrors and the kind of lighting they usually reserve for brain surgery, I find myself face to face with the truth of how impossible it would be to pass as Brad Pitt's twin. I swear my bathroom shaving mirror tells a different story when it's all steamed up.

Changing-room mirrors might show us how the clothes fit—pretty well, in the case of my cousin's tutu, you'll be glad to know—but do they really show the whole picture? What about what God sees when we're squeezing our way into those leopard-print dungarees? Well, apart from a fashion idiot, I reckon God sees a little more than we do—which brings into focus the true story behind the clothes we buy. If you ask me, God sees beyond the storefront window of fashion, and it's about time we did, too.

Sadly, we don't. We currently spend a colossal amount of money on clothes. The United Kingdom forks out more than £2.5 billion per month, for an annual total of £23 billion—which works out to an average of £400 per person per year.[1] In the United States, the figures are even higher, with the clothing industry raking in $200 billion every year. The average American woman has thirty pairs of shoes and an annual clothing budget of a little under $2,000.[2] That's a lot of money, and you've got to wonder where all those clothes come from. In my case, until I was sixteen most of them came from my Gran's knitting needles, but I'd rather not go there. The reality is that more than half of the clothes sold in the United Kingdom are imported, many from developing countries.

THE AVERAGE AMERICAN WOMAN HAS THIRTY PAIRS OF SHOES AND AN ANNUAL CLOTHING BUDGET OF A LITTLE UNDER $2,000.

That means cheap clothes for us, which is nice. But that's not the end the story, by any means. All too often cheap clothes mean terrible working conditions for the people who make them.

Ninety percent of those involved in making clothes are women, working in factories, sweatshops, or their home. But if you think they've got their feet up in front of the television while they sew in a few zippers, think again. Conditions are not always as neat and nice as the finished product would have us believe.

This doesn't just apply to a few people in remote countries whose names we'd have trouble pronouncing—the issue of unsafe, unfair, and unethical working conditions is massive. And who do you think ends up putting up with these terrible wages and dangerous conditions? You guessed it—women and children, generally the most vulnerable members of any society. It's a shocking fact, but one-quarter of all children between four and fourteen in the developing world are out at work.

And what is work like for these 250 million child laborers? Hours are long, conditions are dangerous, and employers often abuse their rights. Workers who produce the brands that we all love often find themselves facing some pretty tough conditions. Besides fifteen-hour days, bans on toilet breaks, and inadequate fire-escape routes, some are subjected to various forms of punishment, including beatings, summary sackings, and withheld wages.

In China, workers need to earn $1 per hour in order to maintain a basic standard of living. The average pay for garment workers, however, is just $0.30 an hour. This means they do not earn enough wages to feed their family, send their children to school, or have access to safe water and sanitation. The conditions at work may be unacceptable to us, but others do not have luxury of choice.

In El Salvador women who sew garments for a major sportswear company work for eight hours and leave with just $4.79. Take away $0.68 for bus fare, $0.80 for a basic breakfast, and $1.49 for a modest lunch—meals that they are forced to buy from the work canteen—and they're left with $1.82 for the day. Since even the most basic accommodation (a 10-by-12-foot room with a shared sink) sets workers back $1.03 per day, there's no way that the final $0.79 would be enough to provide a $1 supper for a family of three. How could it stretch to the $1.13 per-day, per-child cost for daycare? What about the occasional $8 needed for new shoes? What if they get ill? Women sewing expensive $75 shirts for a well-known brand are forced to raise their children on coffee and lemonade because they cannot afford milk. To climb out of this they would only need to earn $1.18

an hour, but who's going to hold out for a 75 percent wage increase?

But while the workers get less, the men in suits benefit from regular perks and boosts: American managing directors are earning 417 times the wages of the factory workers they employ. The CEO of one major sportswear company gets paid $15,000 a week for working sixteen hours a day, while the worker making the sportswear works the same number of hours and gets paid $15 per week.

An average pair of sneakers costs around $80. How much do you think the worker who stitches up the shoes gets paid? A measly $4.26. The world "unfair" doesn't even come close. Or what about those good-looking $75 NFL and NBA jerseys? The National Labor Committee found out that workers in Honduras earned just $0.19 for each jersey made—a shocking 0.3 percent of the retail price.[3]

Percentage of American teenage girls who report store-hopping as their favorite activity: 93%

Year in which the number of shopping centers in the United States (32,563) surpassed the number of high schools: 1987

Average time spent shopping per week: six hours[4]

This is wrong, plain and simple. God's heart breaks when His children are exploited and oppressed, and the Bible is packed with challenges about the need for justice in trade—the need to pay workers fairly and not exploit them for money. As Christians we're called to care and take action to make a difference.

But we like cheap clothes. We chase after the latest bargain as the price of imports plummets. We like good fashion too, or at least we like the fact that fashion moves so quickly these days. Where retailers used to offer four collections of clothes each year, they now opt for a rolling program of continual new styles, many of which take just six or eight weeks to make the transition from the designer's pad to the cash register. Added to that is the fact that retailers no longer want to have warehouses filled with stock waiting to be sold. Many stores want to be as slender as their mannequins, unhindered by the bulk of potential failure. Their solution has been the implementation of "just in time" delivery demands, leaving suppliers with almost one-third less time to produce the goods. Orders are often smaller and less predictable. Finally, prices have slumped, in some cases by as much as 30 percent over the last three years. Add all this together, and you end up with big smiles at the cash register for us, but a serious deterioration in working standards at the other end of the retail chain.

For the business on the lookout for increased efficiency and decreased costs, outsourcing makes perfect sense. So do Export Processing Zones (EPZs)—vast industrial estates created by governments in countries such as Indonesia to attract wealthy global customers with the lure of massive tax breaks and a pliable workforce. The EPZ in North Jakarta is home to thirty thousand workers in two hundred companies, 70 percent of which are garment factories. Clearly, governments are keen to hang on to their assets, and many EPZs have developed a reputation for offering workers no protection of basic rights. Unions are rarely allowed, and prying eyes are refused access.

More often than not, it's the person at the bottom of the chain who ends up paying the price for our desires. Whether it's unfair or unsafe working conditions or cut wages, our good-looking bargains come at an ugly price.

....

Real-life stories: supply and demand

Dewi knows just how much control the retailers really have over their suppliers. She knows the hypocrisy of corporate giants who claim to value their labor yet turn a blind eye to the malevolent actions of their contractors. She knows all this because she has worked in numerous garment factories in Indonesia over the years. She has experienced what it is like to work full time—one day off each week during less-busy times—and still take home less that £50 ($87.50) every month. She has endured verbal abuse when trying to sit down after having stood for ten hours at a machine. She has started work at seven o'clock in the morning and finished at six the next morning when the company had orders to fulfill.

"Eight years working," says Dewi, "has taught me about the suffering and pain of workers in garment factories."

The pain is real and the scars are visible.

"I have a friend who worked in the factory, and she cut off her finger on the cutting machine, as it was broken and couldn't stop. There was no guard around the machine blade. In another factory, two pregnant workers miscarried in the toilet. They didn't tell the company they were pregnant because they were afraid of losing their jobs and they needed the money. They carried on working."

Workers like Dewi are regularly reminded of the only mantra that counts: Target! Target! Target! If workers miss theirs consistently for more than four weeks, they are fired. If they meet their target one day, it will be raised the next.

"You can't win. If you don't meet the target you lose out, but if you hit it you lose out, too."

Suthasinee used to work at a factory in Thailand, making clothes for major sportswear companies. After an eleven-hour day that included three hours of overtime, she wound up taking home just $7.63. She did this six days a week, often working even longer hours until midnight. Inside the factory the heat was as oppressive as the rest of the working conditions: blocked fire exits, a compulsory canteen, and managers constantly shouting at the workers to work harder and faster. But working harder and faster meant more accidents: sewing machine needles through fingers and metal splinters in eyes. The work was exhausting, but once she was at home, she had too little energy and too little cash to go out and enjoy herself. Suthasinee would have had to spend more than a week's wages to buy one of the shirts she made (they sell for more than $50 here in the West). So she took a stand against their poor working conditions. She was fired.

Why does this happen? Why are those who work in the garment industry so vulnerable to exploitation? Our love of cheap clothes encourages companies to put profits before people. As they look around for workers to make these clothes, their eyes rest on those who will make less of a fuss about putting up with bad conditions. These people in the developing world who have fewer choices get caught up in what is known as the "race to the bottom," where the governments and companies that win are the ones prepared to impose the toughest conditions on their workers.

OUR LOVE OF CHEAP CLOTHES ENCOURAGES COMPANIES TO PUT PROFITS BEFORE PEOPLE.

As a country with almost half of its population living below the poverty line, Bangladesh makes a pretty good target for executives keen on squeezing out profits. A staggering 1.3 million people work in the garment industry there; the country is host to more than three thousand clothing factories. It's also a country with a life expectancy of just fifty-nine years and no national minimum wage. Eighty percent of garment workers are women, mostly between fourteen and twenty-nine years of age. With all this trade going on, you might think that this would make for a boom time in the economy. Sadly, very little of the income generated by the industry gets fed back into improving the lives of the workers or their families.

When a bunch of British Christians traveled to Bangladesh in 2002 to visit garment factories in the capital city of Dhaka, they met with factory managers and workers and came back armed with stories of people caught up in the garment industry's less fashionable side of business. They found workers putting in a twelve-hour shift for just $1 and heard stories of horrific accidents caused by faulty equipment. In November 2001, fifty-one workers died on the top floor of a four-story building. The women were sewing jumpers that were to be exported to the West, and when a fire broke out, they ran to the exits but found them locked.

The team met Shima, a seventeen-year-old who left school when she was thirteen even though she wanted to continue her studies. She was too poor to attend, and her family needed what little money she could earn to help them all survive. She came to the city and has been working in the factory for the last three years. There she makes buttonholes in jeans and jackets for twelve or thirteen hours each day, six days a week, in a baking-hot factory that has no fans. For her time, she gets 1,700 taka per month (just under $45). Almost a third of that amount goes to rent.

Shima lives in a slum, which is a dangerous place for a woman to be at night. Theft and rape are common—thirty-one garment workers were raped in the space of one month. These women were walking home late at night from the factories, unable to afford public transportation due to their low wages.

The team also met Rokye. His work is dull, but not quite in the way we might understand. For me, dull is waiting a couple of minutes for a commercial break to pass or spending a couple of hours on a train. For Rokye, dull is sitting silent, cross-legged, and barefoot on top of a long bench with lots of other people, hunched over, sewing diamante beads onto denim jackets. There are no chairs, and he can't shift position if he gets uncomfortable. Each bead is small and has to be threaded before it is sewn onto the jacket. The work is tiring on the eyes, as Rokye has to hold the material up close to see what he is doing. He sews 315 beads onto each jacket, and when he has finished one jacket, he picks up another and starts again.

Surely workers like Rokye and Shima should be paid a living wage? Surely the 1.3 million Bangladeshis and the other 250 million child laborers worldwide should be paid more than is needed just to survive? With some companies turning profits that run into the billions of dollars or pounds, isn't it about time we begin to lift the label on what the clothing industry is really like? And if we've already lifted, but remain inactive, isn't it about time we got on and did something about it?

So what do we do?

The international trade system has the power to lift millions out of poverty and provide countries with a means of sustainable, long-term development. But for workers like Rokye and Shima, the system is anything but fair. Why? Because we turn a blind eye to the evidence of abuse and exploitation. But what if we didn't just ignore it? What if we decided to say no to unfair trade? What if we decided to show the suffering that really goes on in the clothing industry?

We don't just want companies to make hollow pledges or produce some glossy brochure with paper promises that never materialize. All retailers need to sign up to voluntary, independently verified codes of conduct. That's why the United Nations Global Compact makes sense (see for yourself at *www.unglobalcompact.org*). It has been set up to help retailers develop systems to ensure that their practices are a force of good rather than harm.

The Global Compact aims to encourage and support companies to be ethical businesses, which includes working toward ending child labor, forced labor, and sweatshops, and looking at health and safety, labor conditions, and labor rights. Surely we should encourage companies to join so that they will be held accountable for the steps they take to improve the conditions of their workers.

As more companies join the Global Compact, the greater the momentum will be toward companies behaving in a just and fair manner. By pressuring any company to join Global Compact, we send a clear message that becoming an ethically fair company is a vital—and viable—option. This is where you come in, putting the muscle into our campaign. In an age when stores are chucking loyalty cards at us, we want to let them know that we're not loyal to the shops, but rather to the workers who make the clothes on our backs.

There are four main things you can do to be a part of this.

WRITE
Find out the contact details of your favorite retailers and write to the CEOs; start a dialogue and encourage them to sign up to the Global Compact. After all, people running big businesses are driven by profit. If they get a sense that a growing number of their shoppers are interested in the stories behind the clothes, policies might change.

ASK
Take it to the streets. Ask the staff in the stores if they can tell you where the clothes came from and what the working conditions

are like. Ask the managers, too; get them talking and wondering about the supply chain for themselves. At the cash register, ask for a comment card and invite them to join the Global Compact, to show that you care about those behind the products and that you want the shop to put people before profits.

What about boycotts? They're tricky and only really tend to work when they are the express wish of the workers we are trying to support. Sadly, when Western customers boycott stores, companies sometimes pull out of a country or a factory, resulting in many job losses. For workers in developing countries, any job is better than no job, so it's better to keep shopping and asking questions, to keep the pressure up and use your consumer power.

PRAY
As a Christian, you have power and authority in Jesus' name to encourage and to pray and to ask our Father to let His kingdom come on this earth. As a Christian consumer acting and praying together for justice, you really do have the power to make a huge difference.

SHOP
You can make a conscious choice to buy stuff through ethical and Fair Trade companies, and when you do, there are three key side effects: it benefits companies that are truly ethical, it sends a clear message to corporations that enough is enough, and it allows our money to become real currency—we can use it to vote against companies that employ child labor, use sweatshops, disregard indigenous communities, and cause environmental destruction.

CHAPTER TEN

Money: Uses, Abuses, and Life Without Excuses

According to author Keith Tondeur, things are looking decidedly dodgy in the wallet department these days. We are, he suggests, in the midst of some serious confusion. Here's his take on our financial systems:

"There are two opposing economic systems operating in the world today. They are humankind's economy and God's economy. Jesus taught us to love people and use things—our society appears to teach the reverse."

This quote comes from Tondeur's book *Your Money and Your Life*.[1] Now, books on money don't usually end up making that much of the stuff. Somehow we'd rather do something a little more palatable than spend a handful of hours reading about how far out of line our attitudes have drifted. It just doesn't seem like much fun—stocking up on all that guilt and simple living.

Unfortunately, it's all true. The current version of a me-first faith that tops the polls allows us to exist in a world without consequences. We're told to consume and not to count the costs—whether they be economic, physical, or spiritual—so when someone like Keith comes along, telling us that we've got it all wrong, we have a tendency to switch off.

Which is a shame. Actually, it's far more than a shame. *Your Money and Your Life* is one of those essential, deeply spiritual books that demands urgent attention on a mass scale. Without its wake-up call we run the risk of slumbering through a host of abuses and oppressions, a catalog of crimes caused by the way we handle cash. Without change, we will

> The average amount of pocket money for American children—$230 a year—is more than the total annual income of the world's half-billion poorest people.[2]

continue to fall into the same traps that the early prophets spoke out against. Our idols may come in brushed aluminum as opposed to solid gold, but their hold on our hearts is every bit as strong.

We've already seen that the Bible has plenty to say about money —almost 2,500 verses on the matter, five times more than on faith or prayer. Money is important, and the reasons are obvious. The pursuit of it can become our source of self-esteem, our reason for ambition, our motivation to succeed, and our signifier of achievement. The absence of it can present us with emotional as well as physical problems, with repossessions and prison terms at one end of a radically worsening scale. All in all, we cannot underestimate the power of the dollar to distort and distract. All that silver didn't seem to do Judas much good, and in the scheme of eternal salvation, our relentless pursuit of financial gain seems frankly ridiculous.

But is life harder for us now than it was all those years ago? The Israelites may not have had to face the pressure of high-impact marketing campaigns, but we fool ourselves if we believe that it is impossible these days to find an attitude toward money that God would approve of. At its heart, our struggle is the same as that which has plagued mankind forever—a selfish refusal to give up on our desires. Whether it was apples in Eden or bathing Bathshebas or triple denials from Peter in the firelight, the DNA is identical. Self-interest, greed, fear, self-delusion—they're still in play today.

Yet life does present us with some unique pressures. The way in which we are forcibly pressed up against the window of consumerism makes for its own set of troubles and challenges. Spend twenty-four hours in a typical American home, and the television set will be on for more than seven of those hours.[3] There can be little wonder that children, in particular, are prime targets for television advertisers, and as tens of thousands of ads batter our young each year—defining their desires, molding their aims—the notion of what constitutes "success" is given a concrete, tangible form.

It's not just the young who are targets. The rest of us, as we're well aware, were "born to shop." Why? "Because you're worth it," and if we "obey our thirst" in the meantime, well, that's all good, too. We're kept on the string, jumping for the offer of the free phone, the extra-large portion, the must-have accessory without which our lives would simply be unbearable.

We're left on a perpetual periphery, constantly wanting more but never getting it. Jean Paul Getty Sr., one of the world's first billionaires, was once reputedly asked to define in material terms what counted as "enough." He hit the nail on the head: "Just a little bit more."

But is this anything new? Surely we all know that conforming to consumer culture can threaten God's place on the throne of our affection. Perhaps we do all know it, yet sadly, the reality is that we are still walking headfirst into some drastic consequences for both ourselves and others.

....

Real-life stories: slaves to spending

The levels of personal debt across the Western world are reaching outrageous heights. In Australia, the rate of increase is astronomical. In the state of New South Wales, total household debt increased 162 times in the five years leading up to 2004.[4] Meanwhile, for the nearly 70 percent of Australian households that have a credit or charge card, average debt has skyrocketed from AUD 1,601 in June 1996 to AUD 5,162 in 2004. All in all, personal debt (excluding housing) jumped AUD 2.3 billion in June 2004, to reach a record of AUD 104 billion.

The situation is equally dire in the United Kingdom. According to the counsel charity Citizens' Advice Bureau, the number of people who need debt advice increased by 44 percent from 1998 to 2004. The total level of British personal debt broke through the £1 trillion mark in July 2004.[5] One year later, it had increased another 10 percent to reach £1.1 trillion.[6] With all eleven zeros in place, the reality is shocking: £1,100,000,000,000. More than one in ten British customers have trouble meeting their credit card debt repayments, and the level of our collective personal debt is increasing by a stunning £1 million every four minutes.[7]

In the United States, average personal debt per household is $84,454.[8] Total consumer credit (not counting mortgages or home loans) was at $2.16 trillion in September 2005, yet even that is not a record high.[9] Americans use 1.2 billion credit cards and carry an average of $8,562 in consumer debt, racked up in monumental palaces to consumerism. The latest Wal-Mart Supercenters, examples of such palaces, cover nearly six acres.[10]

In our affection for the pursuit of material possessions, we miss so many of the points in life. We find ourselves ensnared by the very things we hoped would bring us happiness and satisfaction. When our me-first faith shuts God out, it creates a world that is small on dreams and small on success, no matter how big the SUV in the driveway. So our attitudes toward money are a little out of line. We allow ourselves to be defined by the culture and end up dissatisfied, disaffected, or dispossessed.

....

Enslaving others

Interestingly, both the United Kingdom and the United States are in the top ten for both national income (GDP) and child poverty.[11] We may be rich, but the gap between those with the most and those with the least is widening. All the time we've been working out how to get the latest must-have product, we have allowed things to get out of control. Not only have we let ourselves get distracted from God, we have also allowed oppression and injustice to march on unchallenged. Even worse, the blood is on our own hands.

The truth is that the way we use our money can help people—or harm them. A simple donation in a charity box can mean the difference between life and death, while a transaction carried out under cover of the air-conditioned shopping mall can be at the end of a chain of events that leads to an equally dramatic conclusion.

THE BLOOD IS ON OUR OWN HANDS.

But surely we're not all that bad? Surely it's not as if we're actively involved in the exploitation of others? I mean, it's not as if we're chucking our hard-earned cash into the Vice Fund, an investment product that specifically targets your investments into gambling, alcohol, tobacco, and aerospace and defense.[12] Depending on your opinion, the returns are anything from very good (in the '03/'04 tax year it reported a gain of 57 percent compared with the Dow Jones Industrial Average rise of 33 percent) to very, very bad (all the associated troubles from such headline vices affect millions worldwide each year).

Yet just because the corporations are not parading their sins does not mean they are angelic. Citigroup, the world's most profitable bank in 2004,[13] was accused repeatedly of funding socially destructive logging and mining and of using customers' money to "profit off projects that destroy endangered forests, displace local communities, and accelerate global warming."[14]

In May 2004 the U.S. Federal Reserve fined CitiFinancial $70 million for its practice of continued predatory lending[15]—taking advantage of the vulnerable by deliberately mis-selling financial products. Citigroup was also accused of helping Enron and other companies hide their losses by loaning money to them in a special way that would reduce liabilities visible on the balance sheet. That same month, Citigroup agreed to pay $2.65 billion, or $1.64 billion after tax, to settle a class-action lawsuit brought on behalf of purchasers of WorldCom securities.

In 2004 Bank of America agreed to pay $375 million and reduce fees by $80 million to settle civil charges that it defrauded mutual fund investors by a process of illegal trading.[16] At the same time, it also agreed to pay a $10 million fine for withholding and destroying documents requested by the Securities and Exchange Commission.

The scandals continue. Banks across the world are accused of creating and sustaining a world that falls way short of God's standards. From third-world debt to harmful environmental practices, from antitrade union practices to the arms trade, our choice of bank can link us up with some pretty ungodly activities. While some banks and institutions are beginning to catch on to the fact that people are concerned about the type of activities their money will be invested in, the vast majority offer little more than vague statements and veiled practices. Of course, they have a key driver behind them: profit. As the Vice Fund proves, unethical investment pays off. The way the moneymen see it, we put profit before people. Whether they're right or not is up to us.

So it seems that money is a tricky one. By abandoning ourselves to a freefall of spending and materialistic ideals, we move away from God's gravity. By turning a blind eye to the sort of activity our investments support, we allow our money to be used to support all manner of practices, the likes of which those Old Testament prophets would have railed against, with all the venom of an enraged cobra. And it's not that God's gone quiet on His feelings, or that He's changed His mind, allowing a little corruption to creep in these days. We've just become better at ignoring the truth.

So what do we do?

LOOSEN THE GRIP

We need to change our view of money and God. Earlier on in the book we took time to explore the need for a shift away from the idea that money is a sign of success. Financial gain is a responsibility, a tool, a chance for us to put faith into action. Of course, it is also a source of fun and blessing, but there is so much more to the story than that. After all, there are more than 250 names for God used throughout the Bible, but when it comes to describing Him in relation to our finances, the most common term used is *master*. It's right, too: God is the ultimate Owner of all, the Maker and Maintainer of all things. He owns everything, from the trees and minerals to the bills and coins we make from them. It's a simple but profound truth that every decision we make about how to spend our cash is in fact a spiritual decision, one that has profoundly spiritual implications.

The big question that looms above us right now is this: how can we change our mindset so that it really is in line with this idea that all we have comes from God? Most of us struggle with the concept, giving the 10 percent when we're feeling good, but certainly hanging on to the remaining 90 percent as tightly as we can. Is that really the way it was meant to be?

By way of illustration, take a look at the following questions and put your answers in the corresponding boxes in the grid. Once complete, add up the totals for each of the three columns, then check out the feedback to see what it says about your spending patterns.

1. How much would you spend on a new pair of sneakers?

2. How much did you spend on your family last Christmas?

3. How much do you give away?

4. How much did you last spend on a haircut?

5. How much do you spend when you buy a present for a friend?

6. How much do you regularly put in a church collection?

7. How much do you spend on fast food during an average week?

8. How much would you spend on a date?

9. How much did you give to the last charity appeal that you supported?

1.	2.	3.
4.	5.	6.
7.	8.	9.

FEEDBACK

It's about as scientific as a Vice Fund's marketing campaign, but you get the point. Column 1 gives you an idea of how much you spend on yourself. Column 2 shows how much you spend on others. Column 3 shows how much you spend on the poor. So, how did you do? Do you spend way more on yourself than on the poor? More on others than on yourself? The ultimate question is this: are you proud of your spending patterns?

It's time to loosen the grip that we have on our wallets, as well as the grip that our materialistic culture has on our lives. Your next step might be as simple as avoiding commercials, chopping up your credit cards, or giving away some of what you have. You might need to get some debt counseling or join with others as you make a stand for a life that refuses to be dictated to by the advertising industry.

SCREENING

We shouldn't like the thought that our finances have a negative impact on the lives of others. We should feel uncomfortable about this; deliberate blindness to the consequences of our lifestyles is no excuse. Perhaps that's where we should remain, too—permanently agitated, never able to really settle back and feel smug or claim that we've reached the summit of ethical living. Like Abraham, Amos, and Moses, we need to ask questions, to take on the responsibility for things we suspect need changing. When it comes to banking, these questions can have a clear form. Ask your bank about its CSR (corporate social responsibility) policy. Ask where your investments are being targeted. These might include bad environmental policies, the tobacco or alcohol industries, pornography, antitrade union practices, or the arms trade. Write and find out, asking the obvious questions as well as the complex, refusing to rest until you get an answer that you think is full and true.

In the United Kingdom, people are more likely to leave their marital partner than their bank. This false loyalty allows corporations to continue to chase down profits as their main priority. Yet the process of screening companies, filtering them out by whichever ethical standards we hold dear, is neither new nor unproven. The Quakers in the eighteenth century used it to make a stand against the slave trade, refusing to invest money in any business linked to it. More recently it was used to attack South

IN THE UNITED KINGDOM, PEOPLE ARE MORE LIKELY TO LEAVE THEIR MARITAL PARTNER THAN THEIR BANK.

Africa's apartheid. California, for example, withdrew $50 billion from the country. With credentials like these, it's easy to see why investment can be a powerful tool for social change. And if you're still unsure, take a look at the end of Matthew 25 and ask yourself if you really are happy denying responsibility for your actions.

POSITIVE CHOICES

As well as screening out the companies we don't approve of, we can make a choice to support those with positive values. By actively channeling our money into companies we approve of—perhaps ones with good labor practices and safety records, organic farms, alternative energy companies, or those who benefit local communities—we start to use our money for far better, bolder, and brighter purposes.

Want a start? Visit McDonald's. Okay, perhaps not the obvious choice, but there's something going on under the golden arches. In November 2005 the company made Fair Trade Certified coffee exclusively available in 658 of its restaurants across New England and Albany, New York. Green Mountain Coffee Roasters (GMCR) plans to source, roast, and package Newman's Own Organics (NOO) Fair Trade Certified coffee for McDonald's to sell in its restaurants across the Northeast. Obviously you need to weigh up all those nutritional and corporate concerns, but the Fair Trade move is a good one.

A Fair Trade farmer can expect to get paid 500 percent more for his coffee than a non-Fair Trade farmer. In a Fair Trade cooperative in Ghana, workers are paid 60 percent more than the national wage. By supporting the system and opting for products that carry the Fair Trade logo, we can invest in the lives of those whose access to the benefits of global trade would be otherwise restricted. It ensures decent wages and working conditions, as well as sound environmental practices. Whether it's your own kitchen or the one in your office or church, making a switch to Fair Trade coffee can, will, and does make a tangible difference.

GIVING

Hypocrisy never looks good in Christians, but if our spending patterns inflict harm on others, it surely takes the edge off the positive impact of our giving. When there are 250 million child laborers worldwide, 100 to 200 million of them thought to be working in hazardous conditions—like using machinery, working in mines, or inhaling fumes—something is wrong. There are eight million children worldwide involved in armed conflict, slavery, and prostitution,[17] and millions more caught up in cycles of poverty and abuse that appear almost impossible to break. These children are working for us.

Similarly, our voices cannot challenge the injustices of poverty if they are indistinguishable from those of our materialistic peers. The fact is that the more we absorb the world's values, the more difficult it is to challenge them. Why are we here? To love Jesus and make Him known to the rest of the world. But how can we do that if our lives have zero impact on the communities around us?

It used to be that the Church told you how to give your money away and then let you get on with the rest of your life. Once you passed the 10 percent threshold you were safe, ready to move on to thinking about more interesting things. Unfortunately, we were sold a lie. Our lifestyles *do* matter. Our spending patterns *do* reflect our heart's passions. Our purchases *do* determine how people and the environment are treated. Our giving matters.

Is a tithe enough? Should it be before or after tax? Our search for a legalistic answer is a foolish one. There is no definitive threshold that we can cross to breathe a sigh of relief and know that everything is okay. There may be times when 10 percent of our income is an appropriate amount to give—sometimes it may be more, sometimes less—but the point is not physical, but rather spiritual. We are not called to give a portion of our devotion, a fragment of ourselves. We are told to give it all: all the passion, all the pain, all the hopes, and all the dreams. Yes, and all the resources, too. The relationship counts more than being able to gloat over the balance sheet.

Can we ever give enough? No. We can never give enough, but can we ever give too little?

CHAPTER ELEVEN

The Planet's Problems

Just when I thought I was making some kind of noticeable progress in the reduction of my lifestyle's footprints on the lives of the poor, the environment went and spoiled it all. There I was, thinking about my choice of bank, wondering about who made my clothes, and sourcing fresh fruit from manufacturers that paid good wages to local producers, when the phrase "Transport Mileage" entered my vocabulary. My organic, Fair Trade kiwi fruit became more than just a bundle of vitamin C wrapped up in a furry, ethically minded package. Its aerial journey from New Zealand meant that it had contributed to the pollution of the atmosphere, leaving me better protected against the winter cold but confused about just how I ought to be re-shifting my lifestyle.

Thinking about the environment brings along other contradictions, too. While many claim that our lifestyles have made climate change a reality, there are strong voices arguing the opposite position. We can easily lobby and punch above our weight by campaigning against oppressive labor practices, but when it comes to cutting back our impact on the environment, our personal reductions are merely small drops in a very large ocean. After all, what good is it if I bike instead of drive a couple of times each week if I am going to get on a plane every couple of months and head off into the bright blue yonder?

Apathy is not an option. It might be tempting to brush aside the issue on the grounds that it is far too complicated and woolly, but the facts of climate change are an increasingly dramatic reality. In 2004, 254 million people were affected by natural hazards—nearly three times as many as in 1990.[1] In 2003, the death toll from earthquakes, volcanoes, floods, droughts, storms, fires, and landslides reached 83,000, up from 53,000 thirteen years earlier.[2] Across the same timespan, the number of natural disasters reported increased from 261 to 337.[3]

While we can debate over whether our lifestyles are solely responsible for the climate shift, there is no doubt about the seriousness of the consequences we now face. The summer of 2003 was Europe's hottest in five hundred years. The death toll was a staggering 28,000 across the continent,[4] and according to Greenpeace, the area of the world stricken by drought has doubled in the thirty years up to 2000. In addition to droughts, global warming causes sea levels to rise, posing a significant threat to low-level islands. Tuvalu in the South Pacific has struck a deal with New Zealand to evacuate the entire 10,000 population ahead of the imminent natural disaster only years away.[5]

World leaders acknowledge the severity of the situation. Tony Blair has said that "climate change is the single biggest long-term problem we face—the evidence is overwhelming."[6]

Former head of the Anglican Church, Archbishop of Canterbury George Carey, takes it further: "A child born in a wealthy country is likely to consume, waste, and pollute more in his lifetime than fifty children born in developing nations. Our energy-burning lifestyles are pushing our planet to the point of no return. It is dawning on us that the life of our world is as vulnerable as the children we raise."[7]

His opinion connects what many suspect is the cause and effect of twenty-first-century life. Gradually we're all becoming aware that maybe, just maybe, we're part of the problem.

We might not be able to see the harm in having a few labor-saving devices about the place, of driving safer cars, eating well-traveled food, and having a fully charged mobile. Our appliances are remote, our laundry tumbled dry, and our showers powered. The trouble is that our lifestyle choices are making a significant difference. Our wish lists mean that we are using more energy. The result? Our world is warming. And as global temperatures rise, ice caps melt. Sea levels and temperatures rise, leading to more frequent and severe weather events. Just as computer models predicted, warmer seas have caused more hurricanes, floods, and tornadoes. As one leading scientist put it, the rise in severe weather "increasingly looks like a smoking gun."[8]

The science behind it all is relatively simple—at least it has to be, if I'm going to understand it. The blame for these changes lies with greenhouse gases. These exist naturally like a giant blanket that helps trap heat in the earth's atmosphere. The trouble comes when the levels of the gases increase and the blanket gets way too thick. Temperatures rise and the climate starts to change. Greenhouse gases have risen in step with our increased production and consumption. The more we travel, consume, burn, and power, the more insulation

Percentage of fossil fuel consumed annually by the United States: 25%

Percentage of all humans who own a car: 8%

Percentage of American households who own one or more cars: 89%

A person in the United States causes one hundred times more damage to the global environment than a person in a poor country.[9]

we unleash into the atmosphere. And, of course, we're not all equally responsible.

In 1998 Hurricane Mitch hit Central America, causing the most destruction in two hundred years—yet it wasn't even a particularly powerful storm. The facts are shocking: 10,000 people died as a result of the flooding and landslides caused by the hurricane. In Honduras alone, 600,000 people had to be evacuated. Yet here's another truth: by the time it struck Honduras and Nicaragua, Mitch had been downgraded from a hurricane. Why, then, did it wreak so much havoc?

Answer: because when it hit the areas populated by the poor, the very earth on which they lived was too weak to resist. Years of bad environmental management and deforestation had led to a shocking range of consequences.

Forgive the geography lesson, but the deal is simple: when trees are removed, the soil is less able to absorb water and becomes unstable. This increases the risk of flooding and landslides.

The deforestation is worrying. In places like Honduras, land is cleared to provide space for cattle ranching (for foreign markets), as well as for illegal logging and general use by ultra-rich property owners. Desperate to survive, poor local farmers then do the same, kicking off a vicious cycle as poverty and environmental degradation spiral out of control.

But is this our problem? You bet. Unsustainable development is not solely limited to Honduras; the whole world bears the scars. Check out these facts:

Every year 1 percent of tropical forest is destroyed. More than half the world's fish species are in danger of decline through over-fishing.

Eleven percent of the world's bird species, 25 percent of mammal species, and around 34 percent of the world's fish species are at best vulnerable, at worst, in "immediate danger of extinction."[10]

We might think we've got progress figured out, but our shiny lifestyles come at a price, and we're not the ones picking up the tab. The richest 20 percent of the world use 80 percent of the world's resources. It's time we stopped living as if the planet belonged to us.

Who pays the price?

"The main challenges likely to face African populations will emanate from extreme climate events such as floods, strong winds, droughts, and tidal waves."[11]

The fact that this prediction was made back in 1997 only serves to increase the strength of its cause. Even if the tsunami's waves claimed lives at the other end of the Indian Ocean, 2005 was living proof that the nightmare has become a reality. Across Africa's Sahel region, thousands lost their lives and millions were affected by drought. Nobody needs to be reminded of the chaos of Katrina.

From New Orleans to Africa, Southeast Asia to Mexico, one thing remains constant: the poor are still bearing the brunt of the changes. If anyone should be able to cope, it is the Tuareg, indigenous nomads used to surviving amidst the harsh conditions around the Sahel region of West Africa. That is, until recently, when survival became a struggle. With less reliable rains and more severe droughts, there are fewer fertile places for them to stay. Today there are no more places left to move on to. There is no escape from the climate's change.

While we in the Northern Hemisphere burn up fuels as we chase

down the dream of a luxury lifestyle, the price is being paid in
Africa and other poor parts of the world. Poverty, a lack of financial
resources, and a largely rural economy dependent on natural rain
cycles mean that the African continent in particular will continue
to suffer from the extreme droughts and floods that are the inevitable consequence of our changing climate.

OUR CONSUMPTION-HEAVY LIFE-STYLE TRANSFORMS WHAT APPEARS TO BE AN INNOCENT, MILDLY LUXURIOUS PURCHASE INTO A NEEDLE PLUNGED INTO THE HEART OF THE PLANET.

While the West ponders the possibility of using water as a fuel for hydrogen-powered cars, in some Latin American regions global warming is predicted to substantially change the availability of fresh water. Across Mexico and Central America there are indications that about 70 percent of the population will live in areas with low water supply as early as the first quarter of the twenty-first century.[12]

Poor people continue to be vulnerable to change. On average, people
in low-development countries die from disasters at a rate thirteen
times higher than those in countries of high human development.[13]
Of course, some communities are adapting to the changes,
implementing their own shifts in lifestyle in the hope that they can
avoid what, for many, appears to be an unavoidable set of disasters.

Where does it all come from?
Such tremendous pressure on the planet has to come from

somewhere. For many of those affected, part of the blame is local. The
misuse of resources—from deforestation to inadequate reforestation,
poor water management, bush fires, and overgrazing—magnifies the
impact of climatic changes. A lack of national policies on these issues
is a key problem, as is the refusal of many impoverished governments
to control the emissions from their fledgling industrial sector. Yet if
these are part of the problem, they are second in influence to the
damage inflicted by the West. Our drive toward industrialization
passes the consequences on to the rest of the planet. Historically,
the industrialized countries have taken the podium as the earth's
biggest polluters. Ninety-five percent of fuel is used in the Northern
Hemisphere, and rich nations produce about twenty-five times more
carbon dioxide per head of population than poor countries. In fact,
the United States alone pumps out 25 percent of the entire global
quota, while the whole continent of Africa contributes just 3.5
percent.[14]

All this talk of industrialization and chemical pollutants can mask
the reality of the situation. The problem is us. Not corporations,
governments, or media moguls. It is our regular performance at the
checkout counter that demands such a high level of production.
Our consumption-heavy lifestyle transforms what appears to be an
innocent, mildly luxurious purchase into a needle plunged into the
heart of the planet. Even one 32-megabyte computer chip makes
significant demands on the planet. To be manufactured, it needs
0.072 kilograms of toxic chemicals, 0.7 kilograms of elemental gases,
32 kilograms of water, and 12 kilograms of fossil fuels. Another
0.44 kilograms of fossil fuels will be burned and transformed into
electricity to power the thing during its lifetime—three hours a day
for four years.[15]

With all this extra stuff, we find ourselves in need—or rather, in
want—of bigger and bigger houses. In the United States new
houses built in 2002 were on average 38 percent bigger than those

constructed in 1975. The average size for an American dwelling is now 210 square meters (2,260 square feet), twice as big as in Europe and Japan, and twenty-six times bigger than the average living space in Africa.[16]

....

So what do we do?

REDUCE OUR OWN IMPACT

The savings we can generate by reducing our consumption of the earth's resources are small on their own. Together, though, they gain in significance. So a decision to switch off your appliances properly instead of just using the remote might seem insignificant, but the prospect of millions of others doing likewise represents a massive potential. Unfortunately, it does mean that you'll have to use your legs, but right now, with our appliances on standby, we are wasting resources. In the United Kingdom it is estimated that by simply forgetting to turn off their computers at night, employees cost their companies as much as £123 million ($217 million) per year.[17] What's more, home computers waste £41 million ($73 million) a year and emit 220,000 tons of carbon dioxide when left on standby.[18]

We can try to drive less. Short journeys produce 60 percent more fumes, as cold engines burn more fuel. While we're talking percentages, nearly 50 percent of household garbage could be chucked into a compost heap. So by walking or biking a little more and by not scraping food scraps directly into the bin, we can start to be like those wonderful Scandinavians. After all, they do a great line of knitwear and always look so healthy. I always thought it was the fish and fresh air, but there you go.

Politely declining the offer of a plastic bag at the checkout can also make a difference. The Republic of Ireland managed to tackle this horrendous problem with a stroke of pure genius. In just five months, the government cut plastic bag usage by 90 percent and raised millions of euros in revenue by adding a nine-pence tax to every carrier bag. By taxing plastic bags, shoppers were soon encouraged to use and reuse tougher, more durable bags, ones that would not take the standard five hundred years to decompose.

With success like this, it's not surprising that other countries are doing the same. Bangladesh has banned plastic bags altogether, after they were found blocking up drains and exacerbating flooding. Taiwan and Singapore are also taking steps to deal with the problem—one that sees ten billion bags getting used every year in the United Kingdom.

Then there are the light bulbs. Hardly the most stimulating of topics, yet their savings potential is immense. If every American home replaced just five high-use light fixtures or bulbs with energy-efficient replacements, each family would save more than $60 every year in energy costs. More importantly, one trillion pounds of greenhouse gases would be kept out of our air, a figure equal to the emissions of eight million cars. The $6 billion energy savings is equivalent to the annual output of more than twenty-one power plants.[19] And all that for just five light bulbs.

Of course, there's more that we can get involved with, from pursuing alternative energy sources like wind and solar power to limiting environmental impact through the purchase of, say, a hybrid car. We can do so much better on conserving water and saving energy around the home, as well as in choosing energy-efficient appliances. Then there's the amount of paint we buy but never use, the toxic chemicals we dump, and the cleaning fluids we end up tipping down the drain. All have the power to harm or help. The decision is ours to take.

GIVE

In addition to reducing the environmental impact that our own lives make—by reducing, reusing, and recycling much more—we can put pressure on our governments to take even bolder steps on climate change. We need governments to go further than the Kyoto Protocol—a controversial claim, I know. Despite the hesitancy of the U.S. government to sign up for what is seen as an unfair system, the fact remains that sacrifices must be made. We need a more rigorous global solution that is effective as well as fair. After all, as the first to reap the benefits of industrialization and as those with the greatest technological capabilities, it's only right that we in the West lead the way to a more sustainable future—at an international, national, and individual level.

As we reduce pollution, we also need to urge governments to help poor communities cope with the climate change that they already face. By joining in with any of the pre-existing campaigns or by starting your own carefully targeted local action, we can influence those who make the decisions that are supposed to reflect our concerns. We can all make positive choices that will help put an end to the damage being done to the planet. Are we ready for the change?

It is in the nature of change to require that some kind of payment be made. Of course, if we are to take on a more selfless approach to life, if we're to turn the vision and the values of a strange world upside down in our own lives, we're going to be the ones paying the price. Whether it's reputation, wealth, or status, we're going to come out of this with less than we might have if we channeled our energy otherwise. Sound harsh? Perhaps, but would you really want it any other way? Is this faith about what we can get out of it, or what we can give?

So change is hard, but it's good, vital, and godly. From the voice calling out to those trembling behind their failing fig leaves to their arms outstretched in agony, God draws us toward a better way. With God's gravity drawing us out, when it comes to getting over ourselves, nothing is written.

Notes

Chapter 1:
The Irresponsibility of Self

1. Unless otherwise marked, Scripture quotations are taken from Today's New International Version (TNIV).

2. I know that Abraham Lincoln's faith may be a subject of debate, but it seems to me that his periods of doubt need not take away from his beliefs. Surely the process of questioning God is valid. Lincoln clearly had a sense of divine purpose in his actions, as his statement to General Dan Sickles, a participant in the battle of Gettysburg, confirms: "Well, I will tell you how it was. In the pinch of the campaign up there (at Gettysburg) when everybody seemed panic stricken and nobody could tell what was going to happen, oppressed by the gravity of our affairs, I went to my room one day and locked the door and got down on my knees before Almighty God and prayed to Him mightily for victory at Gettysburg. I told Him that this war was His war and our cause His cause, but we could not stand another Fredericksburg or Chancellorsville ... And after that, I don't know how it was and I cannot explain it, but soon a sweet comfort crept into my soul. The feeling came that God had taken the whole business into His own hands and that things would go right at Gettysburg and that is why I had no fears about you" [July 5, 1863], *http://members.tripod.com/~greatamericanhistory/gr02004.htm.*

3. I'm thinking here about the events that took place in and around London in the summer of 2003. Called Soul in the City, the good work plans to be repeated in South Africa in 2007. For more information, visit *http://www. soulinthecity.org* or *http://www.soulsurvivor.com.*

4. Make Poverty History, *http://www.makepovertyhistory.ae/2005/08/31/live-8-statistics.html* (accessed March 15, 2006).

5. Jonathan Sacks, *To Heal a Fractured World* (London: Continuum, 2005), 18–20.

6. President of Tanzania calls for 100 percent debt cancellation, February 28, 2005, The Jubilee Debt Campaign, *http://www.jubileedebtcampaign.org. uk/?lid=494* (accessed March 1, 2006).

Chapter 2:
The Problem with Our Planets

1. See *http://www.astro-tom.com/getting_started/planet_classification.htm* for a truly bizarre range of astronomical facts.

2. This information comes from *http://www.school-for-champions.com/science/ blackholes.htm*—if I'd had access when I was at school, I might have done better than my three C grades in science.

3. See Tearfund's document "Making Every Drop Count," 2004. Access it via *http://www.tearfund.org* for more information. There you will see that in Rwanda, a shocking 92 percent of the population does not have adequate sanitation. Such injustice claims lives: more than five million people die each year from water-related diseases (see Tearfund's "Campaigning and Water" document).

4. The UK children's charity Barnardo's claims that 3.8 million live in a household with an income below £242 per week. See "Anger greets child poverty advert," *BBC News*, November 12, 2003, *http://news.bbc.co.uk/2/hi/ uk_news/3262783.stm.*

5. See Nick Strobel's Astronomy Notes, *http://www.astronomynotes.com.*

6. "Factsheet: Child Soldiers," UNICEF, *http://www.unicef.org/protection/ childsoldiers.pdf* (accessed March 15, 2006).

7. UNICEF, *http://www.unicef.org.*

Chapter 3:
Gravity's Consequence

1. "All-Consuming Passion: Waking Up from the American Dream," *http:// frugalliving.about.com/gi/dynamic/offsite.htm?zi=1/XJ&sdn=frugalliving&zu=http %3A%2F%2Fwww.scn.org%2Fearth%2Flightly%2Fkarvsacp.htm.*

Chapter 4:
Our World Is Too Small

1. "All-Consuming Passion: Waking Up from the American Dream."

Chapter 5:
Our World Is Too Safe

1. Michael Lloyd, *Café Theology: Exploring Love, the Universe and Everything* (London: Alpha International, 2005). This book is an absolutely superb resource.

2. The exploration of this imagery is brilliantly expanded on by Christina Baxter in her book *The Wounds of Jesus: A Meditation on the Crucified Saviour* (Grand Rapids, MI: Zondervan, 2004).

3. Ronald Sider, *Rich Christians in an Age of Hunger* (London: Hodder and Stoughton, 1977), 44–5.

4. "Colombia: Churches Speak Out," Tearfund, March 3, 2006.

Chapter 6:
Our World Is Too Vain

1. The life of William Seymour is fascinating. His influence is undeniable, and writing a biography of the man earlier this year was a transforming experience for me. It's bad form to plug your own books, so I suggest that you check out Larry Martin's series on the Azusa Street revival. Start with volume 1, *The Life and Ministry of William J. Seymour* (Joplin, MO: Christian Life Books, 1999). See *http://www.azusastreet.org*.

2. Mandela's words are well-documented. For a full transcript of the speech, visit *http://www.anc.org.za/ancdocs/history/mandela/1960s/rivonia.html*.

3. Find out more about C.T. Studd at *http://www.wholesomewords.org/missions/biostudd2.html*.

4. Perpetua's story is well-documented, but for a quick look, visit the Internet Medieval Source Book site at *http://www.fordham.edu/halsall/source/perpetua-excerp.html*.

5. "Harper's Index," *Harper's Magazine*, October 1988, p. 15, *http://frugalliving.*

*about.com/gi/dynamic/offsite.htm?zi=1/XJ&sdn=frugalliving&zu=http%3A%2F
%2Fwww.scn.org%2Fearth%2Flightly%2Fkarvsacp.htm.*

6. Dhaka City Corporation, *http://www.worldbank.org/html/fpd/urban/urb_
age/disastermgt/dhaka.htm.*

Chapter 7:
Leaving the Personal Planet

1. See S. Terrien's commentary in *The Interpreter's Bible* (ed. G.A. Buttrick),
vol. 3 (Nashville: Abingdon Press, 1954), 879.

2. David Wolfers, *Deep Things out of Darkness* (Netherlands: Eerdmans, 1995).

3. Jonathan Sacks, *To Heal a Fractured World* (London: Continuum, 2005).

Chapter 8:
Giving In to the Pull

1. N.T. Wright, *The Challenge of Jesus* (London: SPCK, 2000).

2. All of these stats can be found in The Millennium Development Goals
Report 2005, published by the United Nations. There are other sources to
which one could turn in order to see an even more dramatic picture, yet
even an agency as big and as politically sensitive as the UN recognizes the
gulf between rich and poor.

3. Ibid.

4. Leo Hickman, *A Good Life* (London: Guardian Books, 2005). This is an
astoundingly good, practical book. Someone really needs to do a version that
is specific to every major Western country, as Hickman's only problem is that
he focuses almost exclusively on problems and solutions for UK residents.
Still, it's great reading, whatever the weather. Find out more by entering *Leo
Hickman* into the search box at *http://www.guardian.co.uk.*

5. Ian Sample, "Climate change will hit least polluting countries hardest," *The
Guardian*, November 17, 2005.

6. "What happens if the world gets even warmer?" *The Guardian* (accessed
November 17, 2005).

7. The data viewable under "Carbon dioxide emissions (CO_2), metric tons of CO_2 per capita (CDIAC)," at *http://www.un.org*.

8. Jonathan Watts, "The Giant Wakes," *The Guardian*, June 30, 2005.

Chapter 9:
What Do Our Clothes Say About Us?

1. Unless cited otherwise, all stats referred to in this section are taken from Tearfund's "Lift the Label on Fashion" campaign. For more information, visit *http://www.tearfund.org/youth*.

2. Jean Sherman Chatzky, "Retail Therapy," *USA Weekend*, February 16, 2003.

3. "NFL and NBA Workers in Honduras: A Report by the National Labor Committee," July 2005.

4. "All-Consuming Passion: Waking Up from the American Dream."

Chapter 10:
Money: Uses, Abuses, and Life Without Excuses

1. Keith Tondeur, *Your Money and Your Life* (Triangle, 1996).

2. "All-Consuming Passion: Waking Up from the American Dream."

3. University of Michigan, written and compiled by Kyla Boyse, RN; Maia McCuiston, MD; and Ellen Song, MD. Edited and updated by Kyla Boyse. Reviewed by Richard Solomon, MD, *http://www.med.umich.edu/1libr/yourchild/tv.htm*.

4. "Exclusive Polls Reveal New Fears over Personal Debt," *Sydney Morning Herald*, August 15, 2004.

5. "UK consumer debt hits £1 trillion," *BBC News Online*, July 29, 2004, *http://news.bbc.co.uk/1/hi/business/3935671.stm*.

6. Credit Action, *http://creditaction.org*.

7. Ibid.

8. *USA Today*, October 4, 2004.

9. "Consumer credit shows slight drop in September," *USA Today*, November 7, 2005.

10. Joseph B. Verrengia, "U.S. material wealth leads to clutter," *USA Today*, October 24, 2005.

11. UNICEF, *http://nationmaster.com.*

12. Mutuals Advisors, Inc., Vice Fund, *http://www.vicefund.com.*

13. *http://en.wikipedia.org/wiki/Bank.*

14. Rainforest Action Network advertisement in *The New York Times*, November 2002.

15. Inner City Press/Community on the Move, Inc., The Citigroup Watch, *http://www.innercitypress.org/citi.html.*

16. Steven Pearlstein, "Don't Expect Fed to Limit Banks' Bad Behavior," *Washington Post*, March 17, 2004.

17. UNICEF, Facts on Children, Child Protection, *http://www.unicef.org/media/media_9482.html.*

Chapter 11:
The Planet's Problems

1. United Nations International Strategy for Disaster Reduction, ISDR, "Highlights of Press Briefing on Disaster Reduction Education," *http://www.unisdr.org/eng/public_aware/world_camp/2004/inter-day/press-briefing.pdf.*

2. Ibid.

3. Ibid.

4. Stop Climate Chaos, "The Facts," *http://www.stopclimatechaos.org.*

5. People and Planet, *http://www.peopleandplanet.org.*

6. Speech by the prime minister on September 14, 2004, on climate change.

7. "Archbishop decries gap of rich, poor—Archbishop of Canterbury George Carey's address," *The Christian Century*, January 17, 2001.

8. "UK scientist slams U.S. climate 'loonies'," CNN.com, September 23, 2005.

9. "All-Consuming Passion: Waking Up from the American Dream."

10. *Christian Herald*, October 4, 2004.

11. "The Regional Impacts of Climate Change: An Assessment of Vulnerability—IPCC Special Reports: Summary for Policymakers," IPCC, November 1997, *http://www.ipcc.ch*.

12. Ibid.

13. International Federation of Red Cross and Red Crescent Societies.

14. Tearfund, *http://www.tearfund.org*.

15. Leo Hickman, *A Good Life*.

16. Ibid.

17. Maxine Frith, "'Standby culture' adds £120m a year to energy bills," *The Independent*, October 24, 2005, *http://news.independent.co.uk/environment/article321720.ece*.

18. Ibid.

19. U.S. Environmental Protection Agency, Energy Star Project, "Buy Products that Make a Difference," *http://www.energystar.gov/index.cfm?fuseaction=find_a_product*.

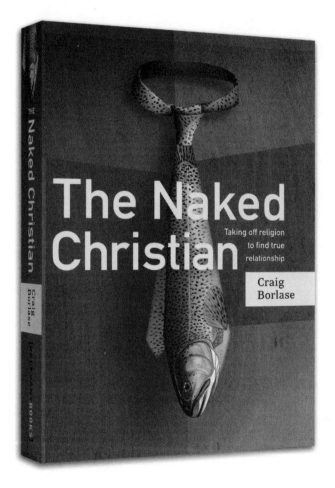